info
The complete t

Distributed by:

UK
A.A. Publishing
(A Division of the
Automobile Association)
Fanum House
Basingstroke
Hampshire RG21 2EA

Australia
Gordon & Gotch Ltd,
25-37 Huntingdale Road,
Burwood
Victoria 3125

 **Tourist Publications**

First published and produced
in Australia in 1990 by:

T.P.Books & Print Pty Ltd,
Suite 13, 3 Moore Lane
Harbord Village
Harbord N.S.W 2096

In Association with:

Tourist Publications
6 Piliou street
Koliatsou Square
112 55 Athens, Greece.

Editorial Directors: L.Starr,
                        Y.Skordilis
Author: Bill Howie
Typography: C.Mills
Design: C.Mills
Layout: C.Mills
Photo-setting: Deblaere Typesetting Pty Ltd
Photographs: Benanji Pty Ltd
Maps: Judy Trim

Printed in Australia

ISBN 1-872163-00-9

Due to the wealth of information available, it has been necessary to be
selective. Sufficient detail is given to allow the visitor to make choices
depending on personal taste, and the information has been carefully
checked. However, errors creep in and changes will occur. We hope you
will forgive the errors and omissions and find this book a helpful companion.

ABOUT THIS GUIDE

The Balinese are born with an innate love of life and a generosity of spirit. This survives despite the inroads of the outside world.

The desires of ambition have been fuelled by exposure to the foreign lifestyles that arrive with each Garuda flight. But are we talking of a Bali of the past, not necessarily, nevertheless it exists. This guide will help you to look behind the facade that has been erected for the western visitor and your appreciation of the true Bali will unveil.

Part I gives general information about Indonesia, including history, culture, government, geology, climate, flora, fauna etc.

Part II offers conveniently described sightseeing both in and out of Denpasar, arranged for both a casual tour or a more detailed inspection, you pick what you want.

Part III consists of a full accomodation listing with useful additional information.

Part IV is full of practical information, starting before you arrive and taking you through shopping and eating, getting around and a page or two for 'help!'.

Part V is a special section for business visitors. Colour maps and town plans have been included.

We hope you have a wonderful time in Bali and that you will love our island as much as we do, honouring its virtues and forgiving its faults.

It is unique and special.

Acknowledgements

We would like to thank **Garuda Indonesia**, the Indonesian airline, and in particular **Mr Barry Mayo**, Garuda's **General Manager** Australia/New Zealand, for invaluable help in providing access to Bali. In addition we are in dept to **Tjokorda Oka Pemayun, Director** of the **Bali Government Tourism Office** and **Roger Hayden** of **Asian Dreams Holidays**, Melbourne, Australia, for their encouragement and assistance.

Table of Contents

PART III – ACCOMMODATION

PART IV PRACTICAL INFORMATION

PART IV – BUSINESS GUIDE
MAPS

INDEX

PART I
General Introduction

INDONESIA AND HER PEOPLE

'MORNING OF THE WORLD'

It was India's late Prime Minister Nehru who, so poetically, referred to this enchanted island with the picturesque phrase 'Morning of the World'.

But there is more to the words than just being picturesque for Nehru had articulated the mysterious and bewitching atmosphere of Bali.

Like all visitors he had been captivated by the freshness and innocence of morning as expressed in the Balinese people whose way of life embodies the joyfulness, the optimism and the hope that comes with the dawn of each new day.

He too must have sensed the aura of wonderment and mystery that is as palpable as the heavy mists that wreath the peaks of the sacred mountain of **Agung**.

But are we talking of a Bali of the past; of a time when a charming naivete was as much a feature of the Balinese as the ready and trusting smiles on their faces?

Not necessarily. The Balinese are born with an innate love of life and a generosity of spirit. This survives despite the inroads of the outside world.

Certainly tourism has brought its intrusions and changes. The desires of ambition have been fuelled by exposure to the foreign lifestyles that arrive with each Garuda flight that touches down at **Ngurah Rai** airport.

There are now aspects of local life that are far from loveable or delightful. The hawkers, the sharp traders and the cheapening of ancient traditions and the devaluing of their wonderful sensuality in the search for the dollar are the inevitable price of 'progress'.

And that is why it is easy to form a superficial judgment of Bali, to jet in and out with an easily digested notion of sunshine, surf and sex amidst tropic palms.

But old Bali is still there. You may not find it readily on the beaches of **Kuta**, in the crowded shopping streets of **Legian** or in the luxury hotels of **Sanur**.

Nevertheless it exists. Look behind the facade that has been erected for the western visitor. Your patience, your diligence and your appreciation of the true Bali will eventually unveil for you the true Morning of the World.

GEOLOGY AND GEOGRAPHY

Culturally, socially and spiritually Bali acts as a separate, island nation. Geographically, politically and administratively it is part of Indonesia.

Eight degrees south of the Equator, Bali is part of the chain of Indonesian islands strung like a tropical necklace along the rim of South East Asia.

This region was known as the **Malay Archipelago**, encompassing modern-day Malaysia, Singapore, the Philippines and New Guinea which together formed a solid land bridge which, in ancient times, linked Asia with Australia.

Massive pre-historic upheavals threw up volcanoes, created seas and separated land into the geographical scenario that is South East Asia today, including this fabled island of Bali.

Beauty and fertility were Bali's legacy when Nature's 'pot' boiled over.

Rugged peaks and deep ravines ease into gentle hills and lush plains on the journey to the sea.

Salt dry pans east coast Bali island

Intermittently a volcanic eruption let's the people know the Gods are still a force to be reckoned with although they temper the fury of their display by leaving an endowment in the lava-rich aftermath.

Lakes within the craters of extinct volcanoes, the deep, dark jungles, the skyline of mountain peaks and palm trees fringing the coastline make the island a visual feast of which one never tires of partaking.

However, not all of Bali is paradisical. Man, Western Man in particular, has seen to that. Industry and tourism can be voracious destroyers and the southern part of the island with that little peninsula that hangs down like a ripe pomegranate about to fall, has seen the result of progress with the jungle cleared for industrial estates, clear mountain rivers polluted with the effluvia of modern Denpasar and ribbons of macadam eating into the virgin hinterland.

And although the tentacles of this intrusion are spreading into those northern areas of the island which are on the tourist route, luckily this is a superficial scar on the overall face of Bali and the general picture of an equatorial island sheathed in the unspoilt jungles of South East Asia is still one that can be believed in.

CLIMATE

The climate is typical of the equatorial belt. There are not the four distinct seasons one would find in the temperate zones. Instead there is a dry and wet season with the temperatures remaining constant.

The monsoons, with their tropical downpours, start in October or November and will continue through until March with December and January normally being the wettest months. The driest period is from July to September although late afternoon showers will often sweep the region.

The evenings are relatively cool although not to the point where you need fires or warm sweaters. Humidity stays fairly high all the time.

Temperatures range from 20°C. to 35°C. (68°F to 95°F) with sea breezes on the coast easing the burden while the hill resorts are generally cooler.

The best time for visiting is July to September with the advantages of the drier climate and with some of the more interesting festivals taking place.

FLORA AND FAUNA

The warm tropical climate, the abundant rainfall and the rich volcanic soil produce a wonderful array of exotic fruits and plants and support a variety of rare butterflies, birds and animals.

A form of natural irrigation is supplied by the many streams that spill down the slopes of the mountains from the deep lakes in the volcanic craters scattered round the island. This is supplemented with the farmers' own channelling of the water into their rice paddies and fields.

Coconuts, mangoes, bananas, papayas, breadfruit, lychees, rambutans, jackfruits, mangosteens, the infamous durians ('smells like hell, tastes like heaven'), custard apples, water melons and the 'snake-skinned' salaks all thrive in the warm humidity and have the luscious taste of fruit grown without the aid of chemical fertilisers. Citrus fruits such as oranges and lemons are also grown but with less success due to the excessive moisture in the air.

Rice, being the staple food, is the major crop and the startling green of the rice paddies before harvesting adds a deep lushness to the countryside. Black rice is very popular and a traditional Balinese breakfast will consist of a 'cereal' of black rice cooked with the local sugar.

Maize is also grown prolifically along with cabbages, onions, chili peppers, garlic, tomatoes, cucumbers, beans, sweet potatoes, eggplant, coffee, tumeric, ginger, cloves, cinammon,vanilla, and peanuts of a surprisingly tiny variety.

Sugar also does well and the markets are full of round, brown cylinders of the coarse sugar which is popular with Balinese and which finds its way into thick, sweet drinks.

The Balinese also cultivate a range of medicinal plants and roots which are used for curative purposes and also play a part in the religious rituals of the island.

The thick tropical vegetation tends to overwhelm the beauty of the wonderful wildflowers of Bali. The rare orchids, the bouganvillea, the tiny flowers on the spiky spider plants are swamped by the dense foliage, the vines and the clustering palms. To the eye the vision is one of green in all its shades and subsequently it is easy to overlook the subtle colours of the flowers.

Bouganvillea and orchids are cultivated in numerous nurseries at **Denpasar** which helps supplement the garden-grown flowers the Balinese use for their daily, ritual offerings. Rarely will they pick the flowers in the jungle as it is considered that the jungle is the province of the evil spirits and hence wild flowers are unlucky.

The animal life of Bali has greatly diminished as civilisation edged its way through the island.

Tigers which once prowled the dark recesses of the interior have practically vanished although there are reports, more likely rumours, of sightings in the hills of the north west. Similarly panthers are rare enough to be figments of the imagination.

However wild boars, feral buffalo, the banteng rusa deer, civets, squirrels and monkeys in abundance are to be found in most regions of Bali. Lizards are plentiful and small 'gekkos' scuttling up the walls and ceilings are part of the daily scene. At night they can be heard emitting friendly, chuckle-like calls.

The most common sight is the sway-backed pig scuffling along the roadsides and amidst the rubbish in the village compounds helping to keep the compound clean.

Ducks provide a similar service in the rice fields eating the insects that can affect the rice crop. They provide one of the most charming sights as lines of ducks waddle after the duck-boy with his white flag on a pole. The ducks are trained to follow the flag and to stay within its vicinity when in the fields.

Bats, brightly coloured kingfishers and parrots, pigeons, bee-eaters, peacocks and the night-loving owls are all part of the exotic natural life of the forests together with a wonderful collection of large and beautiful butterflies, some the size of small birds.

Harvesting rice

The sea swarms with rare tropical fish, barracuda and the sharks who prowl the warm waters. Sea-turtles swim ashore on remote beaches and small off-shore islands to lay their eggs. There is a government campaign to protect the turtle which is in danger of extinction from Balinese waters due to the predatory nature of the fishermen who hunt the turtle for its meat and for the huge shell which is glazed and sold to tourists as a souvenir.

GOVERNMENT

Until this century Bali was ruled under a monarchal system with princes for different regions which expanded or contracted as battles for control were won or lost.

Today, at a federal level, Bali is part of the overall Indonesian infrastructure.

Indonesia is a unitary republic with a President whose authority and power ostensibly comes from the **People's Consultative Assembly** which consists of members of Parliament and representatives from the regions of Indonesia.

The President is head of Government and as such is responsible to the People's Consultative Assembly and not to Parliament.

In recent years the Army has played a major role in running the country.

In Bali the Governor is the link between the local administration and the government in **Djarkata**. The Governor heads up a local authority operating through a parliament in Denpasar and eight regional administrations (Kabupaten) throughout the island, such as that situated at **Gianyar**.

Each administrative district has its elected **Bupati**, a district head, who supervises the regional civil and military administration.

Although further down the scale of administration, but certainly no less important because of that, is the structure of village administration.

The village is organised on truly communal lines with the individual working for the common good of the village and subject to a community system of government and justice.

This is implemented through the **banjars,** co-operative societies of villagers who organise the local life whether it be marriages, festivals, work practises, financial aid and dispensing of justice which can range from simple fines to banishment from the village. However this does not supersede the authority of the overall Indonesian government.

An official philosophy known as **Pancasila** governs the daily life of Indonesians, in theory if not in practise. This philosophy is based around five principles:
Belief in God,
A just and civilised humanity,
National Unity,
Democracy guided by wisdom through representative consultations,
Social justice for all the people.

Public transport

These principles are embodied in the **Garuda**, the legendary bird, which is the symbol of the country.
The Garuda is the mythical golden eagle. Its golden colour symbolises the greatness of the nation while the black colour represents nature. On each wing are 17 feathers, on the tail 8 long feathers and 19 small feathers while a further 45 feathers are around the neck. Together these numbers form the date of the **Proclamation of Independence**, 17th. August 1945.

The motto held in the birds claws is **Bhinneka Tunggal Ika** or **'Unity in Diversity'**. This was taken from the writings of the 14th. century poet **Mpu Tantular**.

The shield on the bird's breast has five sections representing the Five Principles of Pancasila: the star is the belief in God, the buffalo's head is Democracy. the banyan tree is Unity, the chain is the uninterrupted continuity from one generation to the next and the rice and cotton is Social Justice.

The colours of red and white are those of the national flag which consists of two simple bands with the red symbolising courage and the white standing for purity.

EDUCATION

The education system is based on the normal three-tiered method: primary, secondary and tertiary. In the outlying districts children go by **Bas Sekolah**, school bus, to the nearest primary school or the regional secondary school. A university is situated at the capital, Denpasar while further graduate studies can be undertaken in Djakarta or overseas. Although there is no structured kindergarten system young children pick up a wide knowledge of nature and basic living from the 'extended-family' environment of the local village. Even very young kiddies are treated in an adult fashion by their parents and relations and what ostensibly looks like benign neglect is, in reality, an early introduction to the life and the rules of the community.

JUSTICE

The judicial process comes under the overall direction of the Minister of Justice. There are courts of the first instance, a high court of appeal in Denpasar and a supreme court in Djakarta.

The Criminal Law, applicable to the whole population, is derived from the European code.

The Civil Law and Commercial Law, for many years, have been administered with different applications for Indonesians, Europeans and Orientals. There are distinct French and Dutch influences on the structure and administration of the code.

At grass roots level in Bali, the communal **Banjars** administer justice for offences against the village and individual villagers with penalties being in form of fines, loss of privileges or, in extreme cases, expulsion from the village. This communal justice does not exclude the normal functions of the law and tends to cover matters of civil transgressions against the local community or individual members while criminal acts of theft, violence, rape or murder would be dealt with by the general legal system.

COMMERCE AND INDUSTRY

Unlike other parts of Indonesia, Bali does not have an industrial base. It is purely a rural and tourism oriented economy.

The island is self-sufficient in most foods although beef, lamb and wheat would be imported. In turn Bali is able to export rice to other neighbouring Indonesian states and also has an export trade in copra, coffee and tobacco.

LITERATURE

Bali has no definable literary base. Writings from the island have usually been by foreigners about Bali rather than of Bali.

Part of this is due to the climatic nature of Bali. The humid weather of the tropics is not conducive to the keeping of books and records and so the stories have been handed down by word of mouth rather than through the written word.

As the Balinese are an imaginative and a physical race and with their mythology so closely linked to the natural elements it is not surprising that the artistic nature of the people is expressed through dances and paintings rather than through books.

The most notable literary work of the Balinese is borrowed anyway. It is the Hindu legend of **Ramayana** which came from India and formed the basis for the practise of the Hindu religion in Bali.

Otherwise there is little of a literary nature to get excited about. The best books about Bali, as mentioned earlier, are the works of foreign anthropologists and writers producing their own work or editing collections of short stories, folk tales and poetry e.g. Miguel Covarrubias (Island of Bali), Alfred Wallace (The Malay Archipelago), Ahmed Ali (Flaming Earth: Poems of Indonesia), Vicki Baum (A Tale of Bali), Harry Aveling (Contemporary Indonesian Poetry), Adrian Clynes (Tales of a Balinese Grandfather), Victor Mason (Haughty Toad and Other Tales from Bali) and W.A. Hanna (Bali Profile).

Classical dancers

THEATRE

Theatre in Bali bears no resemblance to the Western idea of dramatic production. European-style plays, musical comedies. operas, and ballets are alien to the Balinese way.

As with the normal routine of day-to-day life, theatrical entertainment in Bali is part religious, part mythical, part social and part educational. It is a means of perpetuating the stories and legends from the past whilst consolidating the special cultural identity of the Balinese people. Even though the commercialism of progress has meant catering for tourists few concessions to Western tastes are made in the actual presentations.

Music

Music is at the core of every production be it dance, drama or puppet-play.

The gamelan orchestra is the ubiquitous provider of the lovely, liquid sounds which can be heard in the lobbies of **Sanur's** luxury hotels, at the daily dance performances on the tourist trek to **Kintamani** and at simple village celebrations around the local temple.

The Western ear will find it hard to attune to the subtle differences in gamelan music and the basic repetition of sound, at best, has an hypnotic effect and, at worst, is dead boring.

The word gamelan is from the Javanese gamel or 'hammer' and is a reference to the percussive nature of the music which is performed with gongs, cymbals and xylophone-type instruments. Similar instruments dating back to the 3rd.c. B.C. have been found indicating a long musical heritage whose emphasis on percussion is at variance with the development in other countries where an equal reliance was placed on string and woodwind instruments. However a gamelan orchestra may use flutes and a two-stringed, mini-violin but only in a secondary capacity.

Communal obligations, as with rice-growing and village activities, also extends to music. Most villages have associations in which every musician must participate. Children are encouraged to develop their skills and will eagerly commandeer the village instruments to practise. A child will often be trained as a substitute for a regular member of the village orchestra so that illness or absence from the village does not effect the strength of the orchestra.

There is no formal notation of music. Everything is memorised. This is done through repeated rehearsals and a new piece of music may take months of work and refining before it is considered good enough to perform publicly.

Recitals are popular with villagers whilst in the resort areas tourists will often be pleasantly surprised to find a solitary musician softly playing during mealtimes.

The orchestra is indispensable too when it comes to the production of the puppet plays and the ornate and ritualistic dances.

Puppet Theatre

The **Wayang Kulit**, the shadow puppet play, is amongst the oldest and best-loved of Bali's performing arts. It is not indigenous as shadow puppets have been popular in Malaysia, the Middle East and Southern Europe. However they seem to have been best adapted by the Balinese who used them as long ago as the 9th. century A.D. to promulgate the Hindu beliefs and philosophy through productions of the Mahabharata and Ramayana epics.

The shadow puppet play is deceptively simple: the puppeteer sits behind and below white screen or sheet with electric lamps or oil lanterns situated above and in front of him.

The puppets are mounted on sticks for manipulation purposes and are handed to the puppeteer or **dalang** by assistant as the story unfolds.

Sitting for long periods the dalang must manoeuvre the puppets to form active shadows on the screen, provide the storyline and commentary and control the music from the accompanying orchestra which he does with a toe-operated hammer beating out the rhythms.

The shadow plays, although instructive and often quite philosophic, nevertheless contain much comic relief and a bawdy humour that the Balinese appreciate.

Short demonstrations are often given at hotels or nearby venues for Western tourists who find a full production beyond their capabilities due to the length of the normal performances and the incomprehensible story.

Dance

In the 'theatre' of Bali it is the dance which is the most important component. For the audience dance is the storyteller, the entertainer, the educator and the 'log-book' of the island's cultural and religious history.

Basically the dance can be divided into the two major forms: the temple dances and the purely folk dances.

The temple dances are those associated with the religious festivals and the sacrificial rites associated with such events as the harvest ceremonies. These will be performed in the inner sanctum of the temple.

The most common of the temple dances is the **Mendet** which is used as an 'ice-breaker' to welcome the spirits to the temple upon the occasion of one of the many festivals. It is performed by the women of the village who wear simple, temple costumes and carry an offering in the right hand whilst performing basic movements to the sound of a single gong.

In the conservative **Aga villages** of **Tenganan, Bungaya** and **Aask** where the villagers live a more pure form of Balinese life with restricted contact with the outside world and marriage only within the village, the women, decorated with gold headdresses and flowers will dance the **Rejang**.

The **Sanghyang** is one of the more dramatic of Balinese ritual dancing as it involves ceremonial chanting by a male chorus to which the dancers move with increasing excitement until they fall in a trance. It is performed to help exorcise the spirits it summons up. Forms of the Sanghyang also include a 'dance of angels' by young virgin girls and a dramatic coal-walking feat by a male dancer

Sunset on temple gates in Kuta beach area

imitating the movements of a horse. Sanghyang dances are now regular features on the tourist trail somewhat losing their impact as important temple dances.

The **Barong** dance is also a sacral dance with a similar trance-like ending but it involves a more complicated story and is, in reality, also a miniature morality play. The Barong is a mythical, lion-like creature who represents the good forces on earth. In this dance he becomes involved in conflict with **Rangda**, **Queen of the Witches** in a complicated story about the proposed sacrifice of **Prince Sadewa**. The finale is a dramatic kris or dagger dance in which the prince's followers are bewitched into stabbing themselves - the dancers often falling into a frenzied trance.

Similarly there is a slightly fearsome touch to the **Baris**, which is a mass warrior dance with spears, krisses and shields being used in re-enactments of various war rituals. The Baris is also used as the basis for pantomime reconstructions of old heroic plays and will often include the spoken word and songs.

Gamelan orchestra member

Of the various 'folk' dances performed more for entertainment than religious purposes the most popular one is the **Kecak**. There are nightly performances at a large open-air theatre on the outskirts of Denpasar and various other 'productions' are staged throughout the island. Most of the tourist hotels will have a version of this or the Barong dance.

Surprisingly the Kecak is a modern dance having been especially commissioned in the 1930's by the noted German painter Walter Spies who had arrived to study the Balinese style of painting, fell in love with the natural beauty of the island and its people and became a permanent settler.

The name comes for the 'chak, chak' sound made by the chorus representing a group of monkeys seated around the main performers who recreate parts of the **Ramayana legend**. The dancing is exuberant but, unless the visitor has studied up on the story of the dance beforehand, it can become a trifle boring with the repetitive 'chaks' of the chorus having a somnolent effect.

The **Legong Keraton** is considered one of the most beautiful of the Balinese classical dances. It is performed by gorgeously attired young girls who use fans and their hands in a subtle display of emotion and technique.

Finally there are the various versions of the Ramayana ballet which will be accompanied by a gamelan orchestra and can contain songs to go with the stylised dancing.

ARTS AND CRAFTS

The artistic life is so interwoven with the daily life of the Balinese that it is too easy for the casual visitor to take the aesthetic values of the people for granted. It seems that every second person either paints or carves.

And the sheer volume of work mass-produced to capture the tourism market also undervalues the true culture which has become bastardised by the shoddy goods that are hawked along the beaches of **Kuta** and **Sanur**.

However the real achievements are to be found in the craft villages of **Ubud** (paintings), **Mas** (wood carvings) and **Celuk** (gold and silver work) and in the better shops in the resort areas.

In these villages one can find the cottage industry alive and flourishing. Here the respective craftsmen produce some remarkable work although the eye is overwhelmed by the quantity of goods for sale.

The Balinese artists, colonies of whom live in and around Ubud, share a sinuous similarity in their depictions of the daily routine; don't expect to find differing schools of thought and style although, in recent years, the younger artists have broken away from the pastel shades favoured by the older artists and are using splashes of colour bordering on the undisciplined and the naive.

Subtlety is the keynote of the best Balinese painters whilst the art-collector also has the choice of many works from the brushes of expatriates who have found the lifestyle more conducive to the spirit than the salons of Europe and America.

Mas is the home of the master carvers and their work ranges from small ornaments to heavy, intricately sculpted tables that need a crane to get them out of the shop. It doesn't need an experienced eye to spot the difference between the rich carvings of these experts and the poorly produced and cheap 'souvenirs'.

Silver and gold jewellery and ornaments are to be found in wonderful abundance in Celuk. Every tour company has a 'favourite' stop there. Prices are inexpensive, bargaining is expected and, depending on your taste, a wide selection is to be found. The emphasis is on silver with the gold being restricted to rings, chains and some ornamental pieces.

The highly-coloured batiks are the most popular fabrics and every shop along **Legian street** seems to be draped in swathes of the material. There are also excellent woven cloths to be found in the better boutiques and in the smaller villages like **Tenganan**.

Some of the more interesting crafts are reserved for the temple ceremonies. Women will spend hours weaving small baskets for individual offerings or, for more important ceremonies, tall, ornate creations which will be filled with carefully arranged fruits and flowers. This type of work is not necessarily looked upon as a craft but rather as an important part of the village devotions. This would also include the masks and garments for the ceremonial dances and the tjilis fashioned from palm leaves in the form of girls as part of the sacrificial rites.

In many traditional Balinese households the **kris** is still an important symbol and ornament. Indeed, until recent years, one could judge the economic status of the man by the ornamentation on the kris. The short dagger was considered a powerful physical and spiritual weapon to the point where it needed to be blessed by the priest to make it 'alive'.

The ceremonial kris will be heavily decorated whilst the more practical one will be kept relatively simple.

Krisses will be found in many shops. They are usually basic and cheaply produced being aimed at the souvenir market but, in these security conscious times, if you buy

To this basic profile was gradually added strong Indian and Javanese influences and, in later centuries, Portugese and Dutch strains. The result is an unrivalled race of people noted for their beauty of body and spirit and yet containing surprisingly fiery elements and a tough courage that breaks through the placid facade in times of trouble or stress.

An estimated 3,000,000 Balinese are spread across the 5,700 sq. kms. of the island with the bulk of the people occupying the eastern half.

As with any populous modern nation there is a drift of younger people to the major towns and the capital, Denpasar, looking for work in the public sector, in the small but growing manufacturing sector, in the tourism area or in small private shops and businesses. Sadly, the economy is not able to keep pace with the population and, as with other parts of Asia, it is a common sight to see the young unemployed lazing the days away in the warm sunshine. However there is not the depressed air that you find elsewhere as the general Balinese **manana** attitude precludes worrying too much about the future. The visitor will find it exceedingly easy to slip into the same state of mind.

Bali is a rural-based economy, has been for centuries and will continue to be in the foreseeable future. This fact has as much to do with the strong religious and mythological beliefs of the people as it has to do with the sheer necessity of being self- sufficient.

An excellent example of this is the planting, cultivation and harvesting of the staple food, rice. These are not just regular agricultural chores but are linked inextricably with the cult of the spirit.

Rice growing is an art honed to perfection by the rituals of time and faith. It is a communal responsibility around which are woven intricate rites and collective obligations.

To understand this one must realise that, as with most aspects of life, the earth and its fruits are contingent upon the goodwill of the deities, none more so than rice which is considered the manifestation of the God, **Dewi Sri**, the **Rice Mother**

In the Balinese pantheon the gods have a duality of sex and can be both positive and negative, an important consideration in the day-to-day life of the Balinese people.

Because of this, ceremonies involving any aspect of the rice harvest and depicting **Dewi Sri** will have two figures as part of the representation. Made out of rice stalks the female figure will have 54 stalks while the male will have 58.

Rites will take place at very stages of the rice growing with the first being the ngendang, or 'opening up', which is the first hoeing of the fields approximately 25 days prior to the planting.

The seedlings will have been kept in a 'nursery' section for 20 to 25 days and before being planted in the main fields the farmers will offer up prayers and gifts. At periods of 35 and 70 days yet more small ceremonies will take place.

After harvesting the final, main ritual is undertaken. The village temple is decorated and offerings of palm leafs, rice cakes, cooked rice of different colours, various fruits, roast ducks, chickens and suckling pigs are made. After the food has been offered in prayer the food is then shared amongst the villagers.

The **granary** in which the rice is stored takes on spiritual significance and the handling of the harvest stored there must be done with respect and by those in good health and good standing within the village.

Just as the spiritual side of rice growing is well organised so too is the practical, farming side which centres around the work of the **Subak**.

The Subak is the rural co-operative. Membership is compulsory for every farmer owning land within the particular district. Rules are strict and shirkers are not tolerated.

The members of the Subak under the leadership of an unpaid **Kepala Subak** work together to plan the schedule for planting and cultivation, the offerings and the general daily routines of watering, fertilisation and bird-control.

Surprisingly, this strict co-operative method of farming together with the general communal life of the Balinese does not appear to stifle individualism. It is a cheerful form of socialism which allows ample room for personal expression.

Men and women undertake tasks which would seem, to western eyes, to be the province of the other sex. Women can be seen working on the roads while men will be seen making clothes. But there are still strict delineations nevertheless. General trades such as wood and stone carving and carpentry remain the province of the man as do artistic ventures like painting and writing. Generally domestic duties belong to women however only men are allowed to prepare the ceremonial pork and turtle dishes for major banquets. While the man may carry heavy goods on a pole across his shoulders a woman may only carry such articles on her head.

Care of the children is a mutual responsibility although much more freedom is given than by your average Western parent. There is no stinting of love but the Balinese treat the children more as small adults while still not burdening them with the cares of adulthood (babies,

Temple at seaside

Children Ubud

incidentally, are rarely allowed to crawl because this reflects the actions of animals which are distasteful to Balinese, so the infant is usually carried everywhere). This breeds a child of greater independence and a child who is equally at home with any family rather than being tied solely to his natural parents. In other words the Balinese have long practised the idea of the extended family.

This extended family support was made easy by the structure of the Balinese living quarters. A traditional Balinese home or **kuren** would normally consist of several related families living within the one compound.

The compound was walled and as you will notice in Bali would not have windows onto the outside. The gate is normally at the side and just beyond the ornate carved stone-work of the gate is usually another small wall, which is not to protect the residents from the unwelcome gaze of strangers but to keep out the evil spirits.

The set-up of the family compound was governed by the religious beliefs of the Balinese. It was always built on a mountain/sea axis with the head towards the sacred mountain Agung and the rear of the compound towards the sea. This meant the most important part of the home, the family shrine, the bedrooms and living quarters were in the upper or mountain half while the kitchen, granary and refuse pits were at the lower or sea half. Some Balinese liken the home to the human body with the shrine being the head, the bedrooms and living quarters being the arms, the gate being the genitals, the kitchen and granary being the legs and feet and the refuse pits being you know what!

In Bali the terms 'north' and 'south' are often used in this 'mountain' and 'sea' context rather than as strict points of the compass.

In addition to the main family shrine or temple there are generally smaller shrines either outside or inside the gate and which are attended every morning with small offerings of rice or flowers. The flowers are grown for the purpose in the compound or bought especially from the village; they are never picked wild from the jungle as it is the domain of the evil spirits.

While there is no set time for meals they generally fall into the normal category of breakfast, lunch and an evening meal. Rice and vegetables together with tropical fruits provide the basic diet with an emphasis of hot chillies and red peppers together with local spices and herbs to add a zest to the cooking which the Westerner initially will find awesome. Meats are also part of the diet but they play a larger role at the ritual feasts of which there are many as the Balinese love a good festival whether connected with the rites of rice growing, the annual reverence to a particular god or just for the sake of having a good time.

A caste system, in the **Hindu** tradition, still lingers on and is similar to the Western idea of upper, middle and working classes. However, there is no untouchable class although there is a sharing of the world-wide disdain for those who do the menial, unpleasant jobs in society.

The caste system is divided into **Brahmanas, Ksatriyas, Wesya** and **Jaba**.

Brahmanas are the priestly caste similar to the Brahmins of India and they cover the priests and teachers including the finest craftsmen who are distinguished by the prefix **Ida Bagus** for men and **Ida Ayu** for women e.g. the master carver of Mas is Ida Bagus Tilem.

Ksatriyas are the warrior or military class and bear the title **Dewa Agung** or **Ratu**.

Wesya are the merchants and traders and will often take the name **Gusti**.

Jaba are the rest of the population, the ordinary farmers and workers. It is customary for these families to christen their children with standard, chronological names e.g. the first child is called Wayan, the second Made, the third Nyoman and the fourth Ketut. This makes for simplicity and a lack of arguments when it comes to naming the new baby.

These comments, of course, apply to the basic rural population and those town-dwellers who prefer the old ways. Western influences have altered the basic style of living for many Balinese who now live in European style homes and follow European lifestyles albeit still with a fervent faith in the old gods.

MEETING PEOPLE

Due to the widespread use of English and the natural warmth of the Balinese this is not a problem although there will be a natural shyness about inviting a complete stranger into one's home.

However personal contact is easy to make and the Balinese are particularly happy to chat and explain their practises and way of life.

Guests are expected to bring a present when formally invited to a Balinese home. The present can be flowers, fruits, sweets, clothing, silk, perfume or small items of pottery or wood. However it is not normal to take liquor as in Western society. The gift should always be offered with the right hand.

Meals are usually served by the host even if he has servants. At the end it is quite permissible to belch to show proper appreciation.

It is well to remember not to point with the index finger. To give directions it is wise to do so with the thumb and a closed hand, like a hitch-hiker.

Westerners with white or red hair are often looked on with amusement or awe. Red hair especially is considered by older Balinese as the sign of a witch or devil. However the younger ones are well used to the sight of foreigners with red hair.

Because so many foreign visitors have shown a lack of respect for Balinese religious beliefs and temples and have indulged in loutish, drunken behaviour don't be surprised if the average Balinese, particularly in the major resort areas, shows a disdain for the Westerner. The Ugly Australian, American, Briton, German and any other race you care to name, is, unfortunately, a common sight in the countries of Asia and the boorish ignorance shown by so many tourists does little to endear us to the charming and sophisticated people of the region.

BALINESE LANGUAGE

Throughout Indonesia there are 250 different languages or dialects. Although English is understood readily, and is taught as a second language in schools, the basic tongue whether in Sumatra or Bali is **Bahasa Indonesia**. This is akin to Malay, is written in Roman script and based on Dutch or European orthography.

The language, with so many words for commonplace objects being variations on English, is quite easy to understand visually and to pronounce.

Pronunciation hints:

a	as in 'father'
ai	as in 'time'
c	as in 'church'
k	as in 'king'
ng	as in 'singer'
ngg	as in 'dingo'
u	as in 'full'
g	as in 'gust'
j	as in 'jack'

Basic phrases:

good morning	selamat pagi
good afternoon	selamat sore
good night	selamat malam
goodbye	selamat jalan
thank you	terim kasih
yes	ya
no	tidak, tak

Funeral procession

In both the mythology and the religion there is a strong emphasis on counter-balance: for every good or beneficial god there is a respective evil one. Thus the protective **sanghyang** and **kawitan** spirits will be balanced out by the **butas** and kalas who haunt the dark regions of the forests, the waters of the seas, the crossroads and the cemeteries.

This juxtaposition of good and bad is notably and visually symbolised by the black and white check cloths that adorn statues and are worn in ritual dances.

The range of gods worshipped by the Balinese is extensive and reflect the Hindu influence. Like so many other ancient beliefs and legends a strong emphasis is placed on the natural elements together with subsidiary cults of the ancestor.

The overall divinity is **siwa** who is an abstract 'umbrella' for all the gods. He is God as such and the generator and creator of life however devotion to him is somewhat muted compared to the offerings to the other gods who are part of the daily routine.

The following therefore are the major 'day-to-day' gods who have developed out of the mythology of the island and are still basically worshipped by the Balinese:

Surya......the Sun, and chief god in the Balinese pantheon.
Batara Guru...the Supreme Teacher.
Brahma....God of Fire and Lord of Cremation.
Wisnu....God of Waters, Fertility and the Underworld.
Dewi Sri...wife of Wisnu, Goddess of Agriculture (Rice Mother).
Indra....God of Winds and Storms.
Durga....Goddess of Death.
Yama.....God of Hell and Judge of Souls.
Kala.....God of Darkness, the eternally hungry antithesis of Siwa. A Christian equivalent would be Satan.
Uma......Mother of Nature, one of the wives of Siwa.
Semara...God of Love (in the physical form).
Waruna...God of the Sea.
Antaboga..Serpent Guardian of the Underworld.
Sanghyang Ibu Pertiwi....Mother Earth.

The best example of the mythology of Bali is the famed **Ramayana**, the Hindu epic poem which is popular throughout South East Asia and the sub-continent.

In Bali the poem is performed as part of the **Kecak dance**, through shadow-puppet plays, in song and in straight drama. It is the classic adventure tale of good overcoming evil, with a handsome hero, a beautiful heroine and a suitably nasty villain - a regular rice-field melodrama.

The story tells of **Rama**, the incarnation of **Wisnu**, who, by breaking the bow of Siwa, wins the hand of **Sita** the daughter of the **King of Mithila**. During Rama's absence, **Rawana**, the demonic, ten-headed **King of Lankah** (modern-day Sri Lanka), carries off Sita. Rama strikes an alliance with **Hanuman**, king of the monkeys. The monkey troops build a stone bridge linking Lanka with the mainland (India) and with the help of a further band of bears, Rama eventually destroys Rawana and rescues Sita. Normally this would be the requisite happy ending, however epic poems being epic poems the drama continues with Sita being suspected by Rama of infidelity which leads to the ordeal of fire which Sita passes through without blemish. Even so Rama is still suspicious and in desperation Sita appeals to her mother **Sanghyang Ibu Pertiwi**, Mother Earth, with the words: 'O Earth! thou to whom I owe my existence, justify me this day in the sight of the universe; and if it is true that I have never ceased to be a virtuous woman, accord me an indisputable proof of my chastity by opening thyself under my feet and swallowing me up!'. Immediately the Earth opened up and swallowed the faithful, chaste but luckless Sita.

Besakiah temple

The **Ramayana** was written in the 2nd. century B.C. by the poet **Valmiki** and runs to seven books containing 48,000 lines, so it is not your average limerick!

An even longer epic is the **Mahabharata** which was composed over six centuries from 400 B.C. to 200 A.D. by various authors and runs to 200,000 lines. It chronicles the battles between the five brothers, the **Pandawas** (the good guys) and their hundred cousins, the **Korawas** (the bad guys). It has been adopted into the mythical lore of Bali but has not the popularity of the Ramayana.

HISTORICAL AND CULTURAL DATES

The history and culture of Bali is relatively straight-forward but even so a much longer work is needed to do justice to the subject. The following, therefore, is a surface-skimming project at best and should be read as a basic primer to the events, personalities and cultural developments that contributed in some way to the physical, mental and religious growth of Bali. Indonesia is also covered for Bali cannot be entirely divorced from the mainstream of Indonesian life.

Antique idol in Denpasar city temple

Early history

Accepting that early forms of man developed in the African continent it is believed that **Homo Erectus** moved across to Java and the rest of the **Malay Archipelago** via the Middle East and India eventually finding his way to China. However there is a theory that the Malay Archipelago, of which Bali was part, was in fact slowly peopled from China. This trek took place approx. 700,000 years ago, just prior to the **First Ice Age.**

The first evidence of fire being used for domestic use comes from this time and was found in China. The most notable discovery was that of **Peking Man** unearthed in **Zhoukoudian** near Beijing in 1927.

Peking Man, from the Middle Pleistocene era, is 450,000 to 500,000 years old. However there is no actual physical evidence to suggest that Peking Man's compatriots were to be found in the Malay Archipelago. We can only rely on supposition. The earliest discovery was from 35,000 years ago, that of modern man whose relics were found in Sarawak's Niah Caves. **Austronesian** speaking peoples, possibly from Southern China or Taiwan, moved down to this region via the Philippines. Their descendants were to have settled Melanesia in 2000 B.C. and by 1300 B.C., had already sailed across to Fiji.

Barong dancer

During this time early man started to consolidate his mastery of the elements. The use of tools became more sophisticated, animals were put to domestic use, the cultivation of crops increased, a primitive interest in art emerged, pagan worship took on a more cohesive shape and interaction between tribes made mankind aware of his social condition. One has to assume that similar developments were taking place along the Malay Archipelago.

In the meantime Middle Eastern civilisations were expanding and culturally developing at a faster pace with Egypt, in particular, taking the lead. By 3500 B.C. the first step pyramid at **Saqqara** had been built, the earliest examples of Egyptian hieroglyphics had been etched on walls, Jericho had been founded, the wheel and the plough invented and tribes were spreading through the Americas.

To the north China's civilisation was formalising with the establishment of the Xia dynasty, the first dynasty, in 2205 B.C.

In 1800 BC bronze was in use in China and elsewhere while the first evidence of a Bronze Age culture in this region was found in Malaya where bronze gongs and bells from Sumatra were unearthed and dated to around 250 B.C. Similarly Chinese ceramics from the Han Dynasty (206 B.C. to 220 A.D.) have been found in Indonesia the only country outside China where they have been discovered.

It is believed Bali had an extensive population at this time with a structured village system and funerary system of internment in large jars and stone coffins.

The recorded history of Bali starts around the 10th. century A.D. Until then, as far as historical records or evidence are concerned, Bali was dormant until the arrival of Hinduism in the 7th. century A.D.

HIGHLIGHTS: Possibility of primitive man in the area, 33,000 B.C.; a 'village' society in Bali, 250 B.C.; arrival of Hinduism, approx. 650 A.D.
Julius Caesar invades Britain, 55 B.C.; birth of Christ; first use of paper, 105 A.D.; introduction of Buddhism into China, 150; rise of Maya civilisation in Mexico, 300; Armenia is first Christian state 303; Samoans colonise Tahiti, 337; Bible translated into Gothic, 350; St. Patrick lands in Ireland, 432; death of Attila the Hun, 453; Chinese astronomers make first recorded observation of Halley's Comet, 467; maize being cultivated in North America, 490; bubonic plague in Europe, 542; death of Mohammad, 632; printing develops, 730; China spreads paper making to the West, 751; Viking raids begin, 793; Charlemagne crowned Emperor of Rome, 800; first book printed, 853.

Pre-Western Era

Lack of Western contact and even an isolation from the events on the Asian mainland left Bali as a quiet backwater of the Malay Archipelago. The village society had developed and with that came the rule of an aristocracy and conflicts as individual regions fought against each other. To this can be added the influence and control of the **Javanese kings** who had consolidated their control as Hinduism swept along on its journey from India to Java and then island-hopped to Bali.

It was 400 years before the real impact of the Hindu religion was fully felt with the arrival, in the 11th. century, of the priest **Danghyang Markandeya** who built, on the slopes of Mt. Agung, the monastery **Pura Besakih** which became the 'mother temple' of Bali.

Meanwhile in 991 A.D., with the birth of **Airlangga**, a series of Balinese dynasties were to be established which, despite periods of Javanese rule, lasted until this century and took the country through its most turbulent years during which the Javanese proved to be the least of Bali's problems with outsiders.

Airlangga was the son of a Balinese king and his Javanese wife and eventually took over the throne of the King of Java where he had been sent for his early education. Airlangga appointed his brother to rule Bali in his name and together they built up a joint empire which stressed strong links culturally and politically.

However the Balinese were not always happy with the subordinate role and periodic rebellions would break out to which the Javanese would swiftly respond. Basically, though, it was a reasonably happy relationship with Bali eventually achieving some of its finest years under the 16th. century leadership of **Batu Renggong** who built up a strong, centralised empire which included the conquering of the nearby island state of **Lombok**.

Most of the conflict occurred during the time of the **Madjapahit** empires of the 13th. and 14th. centuries, with incursions into Bali by the famous military leader **Gadja Mada** who was sent to subjugate the king of the Balinese **Pedjeng dynasty, Dalem Bedaulu.**

Bedaulu may have been a real figure but his persona has been obscured by one of the more fanciful myths from Balinese history. According to legend **Bedaulu** had the handy ability to cut his own head off with a magic kris and then have it immediately restored, which you have to admit is a pretty neat party trick. However the god Siwa was miffed at a mere mortal taking on these magic powers and so one day when Bedaulu was losing his head Siwa arranged for it to slip from Bedaulu's grasp into the river

Rice paddies and Mt Batur

which washed it away. However quick-thinking courtiers decapitated a pig and placed the porcine skull on the royal headless neck. From then on the king was forced to go through life looking like Porky the Pig but retained some self- esteem by forbidding his subjects to look upon his flaring nostrils and beady eyes under pain of death.

The **Madjapahit** empire in Java eventually fell in 1515 under the onslaught of Islam. This led to a mass migration to Bali by those of the Hindu faith which concentrated the grip Hinduism had on the island and which has been the predominant religious force ever since.

Seventy years later the first appearance of Western ships put an end to the comfortable seclusion Bali had enjoyed. Life was to change and, as history records, it was not necessarily for the better.

HIGHLIGHTS: *birth of **Airlangga** who created first ruling dynasties, 991 A.D.; arrival of Javanese holy-man Danghyang Markandeya and foundation of mother temple of Besakih, 1009; great Madjapahit dynasty founded, 1292; General Gajah Mada re- unites warring Balinese states, 1343; fall of Madjapahit empire as Java is swamped by Islam; Hindus flee to Bali, 1515.*

Vikings discover America, c1000; Macbeth murders Duncan, 1040; William the Conqueror kills Harold at Hastings, 1066; Chartres' Cathedral begun, 1154; establishment of first Thai kingdom, 1220; Marco Polo arrives in China, 1275; first Chinese settlement of Singapore, marking a dramatic entry into Sth. East Asia, 1349; Robert Bruce king of Scotland, 1306; Black death in Europe, 1348; University of Cracow founded,1364; Chinese traders sail across the Indian Ocean, 1405; Chinese expelled from Vietnam, 1428; Joan of Arc active in France, 1428; Guttenberg prints first book in Europe, 1445; the Renaissance period in full flower with da Vinci, Michelangelo and Botticelli, c1500; the watch invented, 1509; Portugese established at Macau, 1557; defeat of Spanish Armada, 1588.

Post- Western Era

By 1510 Sumatra had been discovered by the Portugese adventurer **Alphonso de Albuquerque** who started the rush to the 'Spice Islands' for the peppers, cloves and nutmeg that had found favour in the markets of Europe. But for several decades Bali was left alone although there are reports **Magellan** sighted the island during his 1519-1522 expedition and **Fernando Pinto** may have visited in 1546. **Sir Francis Drake** even stopped briefly in 1580.

However in 1585, the **orang putih**, 'white man' made his first determined, if ill-fated, attempt to settle on Bali: a Portugese ship from Malacca on a mission to establish a trading settlement on the island foundered off the coast with the loss of most lives. Five survivors were allowed to live on the island by the **Dewa Agung**.

In 1597 the Dutch arrived to start a love/hate relationship that was to last for nearly four hundred years. This was the expedition of **Cornelius de Houtman** who was captivated by the beauty of Bali and the lavishness of the court of the Dewa Agung who had, at that time, 200 wives and a sad collection of 50 dwarfs whose bodies had been deliberately deformed so they could resemble the ornate carved handles of the kris.

The next two hundred years were spent strengthening the links between the Balinese rulers and Holland via the Netherlands East Indies Company with its sorry record of exploitation and opium running.

This was a period when the power of many of the small rajadoms of Bali started to wane and as other rajas took the initiative so to did the island gradually settle into the eight major provinces: **Jembrana, Buleleng, Tabanan, Bangli, Karangsem, Klungkung, Gianyar and Badung.** Today these regions remain as the eight administrative centres of Bali with neighbouring Gianyar and Klungkung being the largest and most developed, as they were in those days.

Meanwhile an edginess between the English and the Dutch had developed as the Dutch became suspicious of English intentions as the English merchant ships cruised the waters of the Dutch East Indies. The Dutch felt the English had designs on Bali for both its riches and its strategic location. The French were also trying to establish a foothold adding to tensions on the island.

Eventually these threats to their power in Bali forced the Dutch to strengthen their position in the country and this led to the tragic, inevitable conflict.

HIGHLIGHTS: *First sighting of Bali by a Westerner, Magellan, 1519; brief visit by Sir Francis Drake, 1580; Portugese trading vessel wrecked off coast on first colonising trip, 1585; arrival of Cornelius de Houtman, first in a long line of Dutch mercenaries and traders, 1597; capital shifted from Gelgel to Klungkung, 1710.*

Mayflower lands in New England, 1620; Tasman circles Australia, 1645; execution of Charles 1, 1649; Taj Mahal built, 1653; American Declaration of Independence, 1776; French Revolution, 1792.

The start of a long Balinese struggle against their colonial occupiers began with a dispute over a shipwreck.

The Balinese had long held to the tradition of 'salvage' - the privilege of plundering ships that foundered on the reefs around the island. This they called their 'reef right'. The Dutch called it looting especially when it affected their own vessels.

On July 19, 1841 the Dutch frigate Overijssel was wrecked on the reef at Kuta when the captain mistook Bali for Java. The local people promptly rowed out to the wreck and took what they could.

This was both the last straw for the Dutch and the excuse they needed in their long campaign to force the Balinese **rajas** to accept their sovereignty.

A mission was sent from Holland to demand that the Balinese acquiesce to the stringent conditions of Dutch rule. The reply came in the words of **Gusti Ketut Djelantik**, the younger brother of the **Raja of Buleleng** and **Karangasem**. The words are part of the folklore of Bali: 'Never while I live shall the state recognise the sovereignty of the Netherlands in the sense in which you interpret it. Not by a mere scrap of paper shall any man become the master of another's lands. Rather let the kris decide'.

The last sentence was the clincher. War was a foregone conclusion.

Despite the immense military superiority of the Dutch it still took sixty years to subdue the Balinese. One of the horrific results of the conflict were the mass **puputans**, in which the Raja and the entire royal court, including women and children, went into battle armed with krisses and spears and killed each other rather than be taken captive.

The finale came with the puputan of September 20, 1906 when hundreds of members of the court dressed themselves in their finest clothes and jewels and with their ritual krisses marched through the streets of Denpasar to be confronted by the massed Dutch army. There is some dispute as to the actual start. Some accounts say the army opened fire when the marchers refused cries to stop. Other accounts tell of the Raja being ritually stabbed to death by a retainer as a signal to commence. Either way it was a complete slaughter with those not being killed by the Dutch bullets stabbing themselves. The dying women contemptuously threw coins at the feet of the Dutch soldiers as 'blood money'. It is also reported the soldiers took the opportunity to loot the bodies.

The Dutch had won but at great cost, mental as well as physical. They lost the taste for physical oppression and lost the respect of the Western world for their brutal approach to colonial rule.

To make amends they took on the role of benevolent rulers introducing widespread improvements in education, health facilities and administration. They constructed

Besakiah temple

better roads and bridges utilising the ready-made network of tracks the Balinese had developed. Clinics and schools were introduced to remote villages and slavery and the infamous practise of suttee were abolished.

The economy strengthened as tourism gained a foothold and the way ahead seemed secure and prosperous despite Balinese doubts as to the effect on their own self-sufficiency in political and financial matters.

But again trouble was scheduled for the small island. Like the dark afternoon thunder clouds that roll in from the sea the spectre of war edged across the horizon and the Japanese octopus was to entangle Bali in its tentacles.

HIGHLIGHTS: *'Traditional' looting of Dutch frigate Over ijssel provokes Dutch anger, 1841; Gusti Ketut Djelantik defies Dutch government and sixty years of war ensues, 1846; royal court perishes in ritual puputan against Dutch, 1906; Japanese troops land at Sanur, 1942.*

China occupies Tibet, 1751; Great Trek by Boers, 1835; Opium War, 1839-42; Hong Kong ceded to British, 1842; Communist Manifesto stated by Marx and Engels, 1848; Boxer Rebellion, 1900; Commonwealth of Australia declared, 1901; Wright Brothers' flight, 1903; Declaration of Republic of China, 1912; World War 1, 1914-18; League of Nations established, 1920; Wall St. crash, 1929; Hitler made Chancellor of Germany, 1933; Spanish Civil War begins, 1936; Sino-Japanese war commences, 1937; World War 11 1939-45.

MODERN TIMES

With the withdrawal of the Japanese following their defeat in 1945, the Dutch moved in again to try and re-establish their colonial dominance. An independent republic had already been established by **Sukarno** and **Muhammad Hatta** in Jakarta on 17th. August 1945 and in answer to this the Dutch established an opposition Republic of East Indonesia with Bali as one of 13 administrative districts comprising this false republic.

This was to bring the inevitable conflict with the Balinese. During the preceding war years a young, personable, army officer, **Gusti Ngurah Rai** had built up a rural-based guerilla army to harry the Japanese. With the end of the Japanese occupation Ngurah Rai did not disband his operation as he could see that it was to be the foundation of rebellion against the Dutch.

With the slogan **merdeka atau mati**, 'freedom or death' he gathered together like-minded men from various parts of the island and led them, in Mao style, on a 'Long March' to the forest-clad slopes of Mt. Agung.

However his forces were small and those of the Dutch were large. On one retreat Ngurah Rai and his men were forced to climb to the top of the Agung volcano and then down the other side.

Finally, just outside **Tabanan**, the Balinese rebels were surrounded by the Dutch. Rejecting negotiations, on 16th. November 1946 Ngurah Rai led his men on a hopeless attack on the Dutch forces in a manner reminiscent of the suicidal puputan of the old royal families. The battle was fierce, quick and fatal. All the Balinese, and there were less than one hundred, were wiped out. The tragedy is known as the **Battle of Margarana** and the fields outside the village of **Marga** where the freedom fighters are buried are revered and become the focus of an annual pilgrimage.

It took a long time but eventually the Dutch realised they were out of step with the changing world and eventually abandoned their colonial interference in Indonesia. **Merdeka**, 'Freedom' was declared in the huge stadium in Jakarta in 1956 confirming the initial Declaration of Independence in 1945. However it was not until 1963 that the final remnants of Dutch rule were removed with the transfer of West New Guinea to Indonesia.

Despite the euphoria of Merdeka, the new president, **Sukarno**, was to preside over some unhappy and turbulent years. He came into conflict with rebellious groups in regional areas of Indonesia, had less than happy relationships with neighbouring countries such as Malaysia and developed an erratic style of leadership and living that was compounded by corruption at high levels in the government.

Sukarno had prophesied 1965 to be a 'year of living dangerously'. It was to be tragically true. The PKI, the Indonesian Communist Party, had gained strength amidst the rural population who were being left out of the benefits that the government was enjoying. The PKI influence extended into the capital, Jakarta, and on the night of 30th. September, 1965 the Communists attempted a coup d'etat. A young army officer, **General Suharto** (the next President) put down the rebellion before it got off the ground and instituted a violent purge of Communists and their sympathisers during the subsequent months, a time that was to become known as 'The Night of the Long Knives'.

This purge extended to Bali. The stories of slaughter that reached paranoid proportions seem hardly credible to those who love the Balinese people for their charm, good nature and placid manner. However, in 1965 neighbour turned against neighbour with unparalleled ferocity and thousands died on the island. It was as though, behind the smiles and easy lifestyle, there had built up an uncontainable tension that needed to be eliminated.

Maybe this could be explained by the natural disasters which preceded the bloodbath.

In 1962 a plague of rats swarmed across Bali devastating not only fields with the new, ripe harvests but also decimating the stocks of grain held in granaries and store rooms. This was not only an economic disaster but was also a psychological calamity as it confirmed the feeling of impending doom which lay over the country. For many months the people believed the gods were unhappy and were planning some form of retribution. Ritual cremations of the rats took place to placate the gods.

However it was not to be. On February 18th. 1963, while the Balinese were preparing for the festival of **Eka Dasa Rudra**, one of the most important of the annual religious rites, initial rumblings were heard from Mt. Agung. Ash and smoke spurted from the volcano and earthquakes shook the island. Nevertheless the people went on with their preparations at **Besakih**, the mother temple on the slopes of Agung. In the midst of the festival, on March 12th. Agung erupted with a full display of volcanic fury hurtling rocks and lava that were to wipe out whole villages and kill thousands. Remarkably, the temple complex of Besakih was left largely unscathed.

Hence it is possible this natural violence and the general feeling of a decade destined to be catastrophic set the scene for the human wrath that exploded in the 'Night of the Long Knives'. Since then the years have been peaceful although quieter would not be an appropriate word. The tourism boom which came to Bali in the 1970's has seen to it that the island does not sink back into those sleepy years before the Westerner arrived. The farmers and villagers who live off the well-worn tourist track have been lucky enough to keep their old ways. For the others it has meant adapting and learning the modern ways. It will take history to confirm whether this is eventually for the good of Bali.

HIGHLIGHTS: *Declaration of Independence, 1945; Battle of Margarana and death of Gusti Ngurah Rai, 1946; Merdeka and the departure of the Dutch from the main islands, 1956; Rat plague, 1962; Mt. Agung volcanic eruption, 1963; Communist uprising and 'Night of the Long Knives', 1968; Tourism boom commences, 1970's.*

Declaration of People's Republic of China, 1949; death of Stalin, 1953; building of Berlin Wall, 1961; Yuri Gagarin, first man in space, 1961, John F. Kennedy assassinated, 1963; Chinese Cultural Revolution, 1966; Man on the moon, 1969; U.S. withdraws from Vietnam, 1973; Watergate, 1974.death of Mao, 1976; Shah of Iran deposed, 1979; Iran - Iraq war commences, 1982; Tienamen Square massacre, 1989.

TOURISM

As mentioned above tourism's is Bali's breadwinner. The whole island is geared to serve the visitor. Modern hotels, modest cottages and 'home stay' private accommodation or losmans are to be found in abundance. Popular beach resorts are lined with packed shopping streets while entire villages will devote themselves to a particular craft for sale to tourists.

Being within a few hours of Sydney, Melbourne and Perth and with the benefit of cheap air fares and inexpensive accommodation, Bali has long been the playground for Australians and, in recent years, has also been discovered by the Japanese tourist.

Distance has been a factor in the slow expansion of the European market, with the exception of the Dutch and Germans, but this is now developing.

Organised tourism has been in Bali since the 1920's. As early as 1937 the Mexican-born author Miguel Covarrubias, whose book 'Island of Bali' is accepted as the definitive work on the Balinese lifestyle, was bemoaning the effects of tourism on the people and the island's fledgling resources.

By 1940 Bali was attracting 250 visitors a month not including those who would come ashore for a day or two from the cruise ships that anchored in its waters, such as the Stella Polaris, Lurline, Franconia and Empress of Britain (today that figure would be in the tens of thousands).

The entrepreneurial spirit was thriving even in those early days. Not only were there the foreign opportunists such as M.J. Minas and Andre Roosevelt who haunted the wharves picking up passengers from the regular visits of the K.P.M. ships but also there was the indigenous variety of whom the most famous was **Mah Patimah** a local princess' who had been the wife of the **Dewa Agung**, the king of Bali.

Upon the death of the husband, it was customary in the Hindu religion for the wives to throw themselves on the funeral pyre of the dead husband in the horrific rite of **suttee**. Patimah wisely avoided this but, at the same time, brought down the wrath and ostracism of her relations. So without the benefit of the lifestyle to which she had become accustomed she saw the benefits of catering to the tourist and would paddle out to meet the visiting ships waving a bunch of flowers and a bottle having misunderstood the crude American phrase 'shake the bottle'.

Patimah was shrewd enough and skillful enough to persuade the visitors from these ships to use her fleet of cars to tour the bumpy roads of the island and soon built up a thriving trade and an eccentric reputation.

Similarly an Anglo-American woman by the name of **Manx** also saw the potential and built the first beach hotel at **Kuta**. Cheekily she would haunt the well- established Bali Hotel and lure away the passengers booked in there by K.P.M. She must have found this activity good practise for later as Miss Manx then built up an even less enviable reputation as **'Surabaya Sue'**, the Indonesian equivalent of 'Tokyo Rose' with her propaganda broadcasts for the Japanese during World War II.

However it was K.P.M., the Dutch Steamship Line, who were the basic developers of tourism to Bali having originally brought the first paying visitors on their cargo ships which called into **Buleleng** to take on copra, coffee, cattle and pigs.

As the people trade increased so did K.P.M.'s activities with the company buying the government rest-house in Denpasar which became the Bali Hotel and then moving further afield to acquire the rest-house in the mountain

resort of Kintamani.

Air travel came to Bali in the 1930's with an ill-fated airport being built at **Bukit** and which could only be used in calm weather.

In 1938 a new airport was built at **Tuban** where the present **Ngurah Rai** airport is situated. K.N.I.L.M. (the forerunner of KLM Airlines) used Bali as a stop on their long, weekly flight from Holland to Australia.

From those early days the tourism business burgeoned helped along by the western authors and artists who became enchanted with the Balinese way of life and propagated the message throughout the world via their writings and paintings.

Transport problems are now a thing of the past. Bali is serviced by the Indonesian flag-carrier, **GARUDA INDONESIA,** set up in 1949 with the financial and technical assistance of KLM before the Dutch carrier's interests were taken over by the Indonesian government.

Within Bali most visitors use the regular tourist coach trips for the island's major trips, or taxis or 'bemos' (small 4WD wagons) around the resort areas. Local bus services operate between the major towns.

Rented jeep

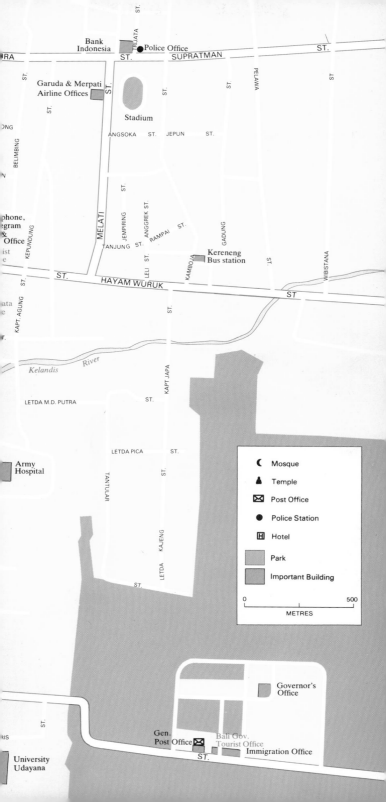

Along the eastern side of the square on **Jalan Nusa Indah** is the excellent Bali Museum. This was built by the Dutch in 1932 during their 'benevolent dictatorship' days.

The museum was constructed along traditional Balinese lines incorporating the features of a temple and a palace. There are the split gates of a highly-carved design, the outer and inner courtyards and the kulkul or bell tower. The main buildings are individually styled after various regional palaces such as the **Karangasem palace** of east Bali, the **Tabanan palace** of West Bali and the **Singaraja** of northern Bali. Thus the museum becomes representative of Bali as a whole.

Inside is an interesting collection of Balinese artifacts including some stone tools from the Neolithic Age, funerary jars and ceremonial masks.

Adjoining the Museum is the **Pura Jagatnatha**, a temple dedicated to **Sanghyang Widi**, the Supreme God. Surrounded by high walls with several ornately entrances this appears to be the busiest and most popular of all the temples in Denpasar. Rarely does a week go by without some lavish festival and it is also a scene of daily visits by the locals. A stricter dress code is applied here than at other temples and there seems a reluctance to welcome foreigners while festivals are in progress.

INFOTIP: It's essential to respect Balinese religious traditions. When visiting temples ensure you wear modest clothes. No low necklines for women and no shorts for men or women. Menstruating women are requested not to visit temples.

Directly opposite, across the green fields of Puputan Square are the long buildings of the military administration.

Jalan Surapati, the road which runs along the northern edge of Puputan Square, as it heads west becomes **Jalan Gajah Mada** once the main shopping street of Denpasar but now just one of many due to the expansion of the city. But it is here, where the road crosses the murky waters of the **Badung River**, that you'll find the **Pasar Badung**, the main market of Denpasar.

Once the market used to occupy open-air stalls along the bank on the other side of the river but the market proper, with its fruit and vegetable stalls, has now been moved under cover on the western side although there are still many stalls selling general consumer goods and clothes outside You need to hunt for the market as the tiny entrances are underneath the Kumbasari Shopping Centre.

Monkeys, Sangeh Forest area

Inside it is a cool, dim respite from the sunshine and smells of the river outside. The narrow aisles wander between benches piled high with a mouth-watering range of tropical fruits, dried fish, peanuts and cashews, yellow cobs of corn, krupels or prawn crackers, mung beans, rice,spices of every description, general groceries and solid, brown cylinders of the unrefined Bali sugar. Pots and pans fill any remaining space. Surprisingly it is relatively quiet here - there is none of the shouting and hullabaloo of other markets in the East. The Balinese are more restrained in their trading. Outside you will find other food stalls scattered through the laneways near the shopping centre.

> **INFOTIP:** Local markets are fun places to visit and shop. However be aware of prices as foreigners will always be charged more than locals. Haggle if the price seems excessive.

A night market operates from late at night until dawn as the women from nearby districts bring in their produce to sell before the main market gets under way with fresh produce brought in at sunrise.

Pasur Badung is the most interesting shopping area in Denpasar. The other streets offer the normal gamut of

Denpasar traffic

shops and services you would expect to find in any city although book lovers will find good book shops practically non-existent although there are one or two in the Kuta area.

Other markets of interest are the art dealer's market, the **Pasar Satria** on the corner of **Jalan Nakula** and **Jalan Veteran** (bargains in craftwork are to be had although watch out for 'seconds') and nearby, the **Pasar Burung**, the bird market.

The **Pasar Malamor** 'night market', is very popular and there are several around Denpasar including one under the walls of the impressive **Sports Stadium** on **Jalan Angsoka**. These night markets are often just a collection of food stalls where the local people meet to eat, drink and gossip in the cool of the evening. Although the aromas from the food cooking on the small charcoal fires are extremely tempting, 'unseasoned' foreign visitors are advised to avoid the lure and subsequent gastric upsets.

INFOTIP: 'Bali-Belly' is notorious but can be easily avoided. Eat only in restaurants that are well patronised (usually no problem in main tourist centes), avoid eating from roadside stalls and be wary of fruit you can't peel and salads (at major hotels and resorts there is normally no problem).

Classical dancers

Denpasar

On the road to **Sanur** is the splendid **Art Centre** set amidst attractive grounds of lawns and pools. Exhibitions of art and dance are given here and regular recitations from Balinese lore are also presented. The Art Centre is the focal point for the annual **Arts Festival**, which runs through the months of June and July and incorporates the full spectrum of Balinese art: dance, music, painting, carving and literature.

A permanent exhibition of Balinese handicrafts is on display at the Regional Trade Office and while the exhibition is mainly for overseas importers the serious student of handicrafts will find it a worthwhile visit and the staff equipped to provide any information needed. The Trade Office is on **Jalan Kamboja**.

Lovers of the beautiful and intricate Balinese dance can make arrangements to visit the two major institutions of dance instruction, **Akademi Seni Tari Indonesia** (ASTI) and **Konservatori Kerawitan** (Kokar).

Young man carrying items for sale, Ubud

Sanur beach coastline

as air travel increased in popularity and with Bali being only five or six hours flying time from the main Australian cities of Melbourne and Sydney it was the logical destination for Australians who found it cheaper to holiday in Bali than within their own country.

Sanur became the alternative destination to **Kuta**. Whereas Kuta found a rough and ready market amongst the young, the family groups turned to Sanur where the location with its beach lagoon's safe swimming for the children and a quieter, unhurried pace of life set amidst palms and tropic gardens had instant appeal - an appeal Sanur has maintained despite the incredible growth of the area.

Even in the last decade Sanur has undergone a face-lift and an 'urbanisation' that is surprising to the visitor returning after a long absence. The once quiet **Jalan Tanjung Sari** which sleepily wound its way parallel to the beach amidst small plantations of coconut and banana palms and where you could amble along the road itself without any great fear of traffic now busily hums with the bemos, cars and motorbikes and the paved footpaths are lined with fashionable shops selling beachwear and souvenirs.

Sunrise Sanur Beach

Off the road though the hotels and cottages still retain an air of seclusion and drowsy afternoons soaking up the sun on the sands of Sanur is balm for the harried soul.

The main part of Sanur starts at the Bali Beach Hotel which has become something of a village in its own right with the spread of the hotel complex ranging from the main, multi-storey building to individual cottages set amidst park-like grounds. The road which once was the main access to the rest of the Sanur strip is now bordered on the other side by a golf course and has been closed to through traffic.

This means continuing along the newly built highway which links Sanur directly with the airport and **Nusa Dua** at the southern tip of the island and then turning off the highway towards the sea at **Jalan Segara**. This will get you onto the old beach road, **Jalan Tanjung Sari**, which runs along the back of the beach-front properties and continues on down to the Sanur Beach hotel.

All Sanur's hotels, beach cottages and better restaurants are along the Jalan Tanjung Sari.

Don't be surprised at signs proclaiming the 'Swastika Restaurant'. It is not an enclave of ageing ex-Nazis but refers to the symbol which is one of the sacred signs of Buddhism.

Similarly another restaurant has the sign 'Bali Yobbo' which one assumes shows a sense of humour on the proprietor's part rather than being a commentary on the clientele!

An interesting side trip from Sanur is in a **prahu**, a canoe with distinctive triangular sails. This will take you across the waters of the lagoon, through the reef and to **Serangan, 'Turtle Island'**. This was named for the number of turtles caught there and eventually killed for the ceremonial feasts. The shells of the hapless turtles are often seen for sale in souvenir shops and stalls but the government, realising the devastation done to turtle numbers by the uninhibited slaughter, now has an education campaign urging tourists not to buy the endangered species. Many countries ban their import anyway.

Serangan has a sea temple, **Pura Sakenan**, which is noted for its pyramid-shaped shrines which are unique. Three day festivals every six months provide a wonderful opportunity to see rare rituals if you have the good luck to be in the vicinity at the time. These festivals include a special water procession carrying large puppet figures from the mainland to the island. Serangan is also popular with kite flyers who have greater freedom here away from the dangerous power-lines on the mainland.

Incidentally on the road between Sanur and Denpasar

there are numerous orchid and bouganvillea nurseries. They supply the Balinese need for floral temple decorations and offerings as it is considered unlucky to pick wild flowers from the jungle due to the bad spirits who live there.

INFOTIP: Bali offers a choice of resorts appealing to different lifestyles and pockets. **Kuta** is for the budget conscious and basically for the young and the singles market. **Sanur** is for the families and those looking for something quieter. **Nusa- Dua** is for the Yuppies and those who can't forgo the pleasure of international luxury. **Ubud** is for the discerning and the lovers of rural Bali.

Kuta

The most obvious effect of tourism on the island can be seen at Kuta which is to the south of Sanur on the opposite side on the Western coast.

Once a small fishing village Kuta is now the very antithesis of what many expect Bali to be. It is crowded, noisy and dusty, only pausing to catch its breath in the silent hours of the morning awakening with another burst when the sun comes up.

And if the 'blame' can be laid at any one's feet, then, in this case, it would be at the feet that grip the surf-boards whose introduction to Bali's waters has made such a dramatic impact not only physically but sociologically.

The tourism that followed in the wake of the surfers brought with it great changes as hotels, shops and restaurants sprouted like rice after a good rainfall. Socially it changed the nature of many of the local people who quickly realised the value of the dollar, the pound, the deutschmark and the franc and developed a shrewd sense of worth and an uncharacteristic suspicion brought on by the less than lovely behaviour of this fresh bunch of foreign 'invaders'. A new competitive edge emerged and an understandable cynicism can be sensed. However nothing can completely ruin the basic charm of the Balinese people, even at Kuta.

As one tourism official explained the attractions of Bali, and in particular Kuta, are the five 's's': sun, sand, surf, sex and smoke - this latter a reference to a fondness for marijuana by the surfing fraternity until the authorities made a determined crackdown on the lads with the strange cigarettes and the funny smiles.

Besakiah temple

For centuries Kuta had slumbered in the sunshine, the waves pounding on to its wide beaches undisturbed except for the prahus of fisherman who would set out in the cooler hours of morning and evening to gather their catches. In the thatched huts in the shade of the tall coconut palms worked metal smiths while in the fields farmers grew vegetable and rice crops.

Europe made its presence felt in 1826 with the arrival in Kuta of the Dutch **Captain Wetters** who set up a trading post. Due to lack of success this was closed down five years later.

If the people of Kuta thought they had a reprieve then it was only a brief one as within eight years another Dutch vessel arrived with construction materials for a more permanent settlement. Also on board was, believe it or not, a rhinoceros a gift for the **Dewa Agung** at **Klungkung**. At least the Dewa fared better with his unique present as his neighbour, the Raja of Badung, had requested cannon and lead and received nothing.

A minor establishment lingered on here without any major impact until the arrival in 1839 of another European, the Danish trader **Mads Lange**. Lange took over the trading post by the **Dawan River**, which flowed into the sea near Kuta, and expanded the trading operations.

Food seller in Kuta beach area

Lange brought European style to Bali. As he prospered so did his way of living. He built a gracious home with a music room, billiards room and a wine cellar. His cooks were trained in Balinese, Chinese and European cuisine to cater for Lange's two wives, three brothers and a never-ending stream of visiting house guests.

Lange is also credited with introducing Bali's first currency gradually changing the system of barter over to one of cash.

Eventually Lange was to fall foul of the greed of the Dutch who forced independent traders, like Lange, out of business. He returned to Denmark where he died in 1856 but his brothers are buried in Kuta in the cemetery near the Kuta night market.

Sixty years were to pass before tourism raised its multi-hued head in Kuta. This came in the 1920's with the opening of a small beach hotel by the American Robert Koke and his partner Miss Manx, the infamous **'Surabaya Sue'** of later Japanese propaganda broadcasts.

However with Sanur being closer to the harbour where the cruise ships docked and with Denpasar as the capital nearby, Kuta was not an immediate success.

It took the interest of surfers in the 1960's to put Kuta on the map. This was the time of the 'flower children' looking for alternative lifestyles and the surfers always seeking new waves and new beaches.

Somehow the word filtered out that Kuta's beaches offered great surfing, that accommodation was cheap and that there was no interference with those wanted to 'turn on and drop out'. Suddenly Kuta was a forest of surfboards, beards, long hair and thongs.

Accommodation was no problem. 'Home stays' or losmans could be had for what amounted to little more than small change to a Westerner even if it meant showering with a bucket and sharing a room.... and meals would be included.

Living was easy, the sun was warm and the tropical setting was a bonus.

Inevitably the word spread beyond the hippy set and regular tourists started to take an interest attracted particularly by the inexpensive lodgings. But they also preferred more comfort so hotels were built to cater for the new demand.

Kuta, however, is not as classy a resort as Sanur. It was, is and always will be basically a resort for the young and those looking for a bargain holiday, although there are several up - market properties like the Oberoi and the Pertamina Cottages.

Food seller on Kuta beach

The Kuta area, which also embraces the next-door beach, **Legian**, covers a strip of sand about two kilometres long linked by several busy side streets with the main shopping thoroughfare **Jalan Legian** which runs parallel with the beach approx. 500 metres away.

Jalan Legian is the 'Broadway' of Bali. It has the best shops, row after row of restaurants, night clubs, bars, art galleries, craft stores and a traffic problem to boot. The canny shopper wishing to avoid the daily throngs would be advised to go there when the shops open, which can vary between 9 am and 10 am. Most of the tourists are sleeping off the excesses of the previous night and it is normally fairly quiet at this time apart from the family groups. You will notice a predominance of white tiles in the shops: somebody must have cornered the market on white tiles for every second doorway opens onto a gleaming, hospital-like interior.

Traffic is a hazard as the streets here are very narrow and there are no pedestrian crossings or traffic lights. Any form of police traffic control is seemingly ineffectual.

There is little of cultural interest here but sometimes down side streets you will come across a small temple or a home built in the traditional style. Near the Bali Oberoi hotel is the most important temple in the area, the **Peti**

Lake Kintamani

Tenget, an historic sea temple which is said to contain a magic box left by the Hindu-Javanese priest, **Danghyang Nirartha**. This temple is much revered by the Balinese because of its attractions for various spirits. One such spirit, the goddess of the sea, is said to take for herself one victim a year from amongst those who enter Kuta's waters. Westerners put this down to the strong undertow that operates here. So, whether surfing or swimming, take heed of the notices posted along the beach and swim between the flags. Generally the beach is patrolled.

Eating is good and there is a wide variety of cuisines. There are several pleasant restaurants like the Southern Cross where the open windows let in the breezes and views of the ocean and where they serve a really cold beer. Prices everywhere are remarkably low. Nevertheless take notice of the oft-given advice and avoid buying food from small roadside stalls; stay with restaurants that look well patronised.

It is also wise to remember that the term 'cottages' is used indiscriminately to describe most forms of accommodation. In many cases 'cottages' are normal hotel blocks so when booking direct or through a travel agent ensure that the accommodation is in bungalow form if that is what you are looking for. This applies not only to Kuta but all over Bali.

> **INFOTIP:** It is not unsual to find older Balinese will avoid swimming in the sea due to the ancient myths of the demons which live in the ocean. Younger Balinese have no such qualms.

Nusa Dua

Nusa Dua is an excellent example of how tourism can generate the most remarkable changes.

The name has come from the two islands off the shores of this tip of the southern peninsula, known as **Bukit**: Nusa means 'islands' and Dua is 'two'.

Although the forests of Bukit Peninsula were the hunting grounds of the **Raja of Badung** the southern tip was a dismal area of mangrove swamps with few people apart from a tiny fishing enclave. The soil was not good enough to support agriculture and Nusa Dua seem destined to remain isolated and ignored.

However the Indonesian government had the foresight to realise its tourist potential. Their move was prompted by the government's concern at the rapid growth of the tourism industry in the popular beach resorts of Sanur and Kuta and its spread into the mountains and to villages such as **Ubud**. The effect upon the culture of Bali was causing apprehension amongst officials and following a survey by the World Bank the region of Nusa dua was selected as the logical place in which to develop the expanded tourist facilities needed on the island while minimising the 'cultural shock'.

Fishing boats on Nusa Dua beach

Plans were drawn up in the 1970's, a highway (the best road in Bali) was built to link the island's tip with the airport, Kuta and Sanur and the first hotel, the **Nusa Dua Hotel** was built by the Aerowisata chain, a division of the Indonesian airline, Garuda. This was soon followed by the **Putri Bali hotel**, the **Bali Sol Hotel** and then, the final 'imprimatur', **Club Med**.

The result is quite stunning. The highway ends at two huge and lavishly carved Balinese gates at the entrance to the Nusa Dua Hotel. The road then winds through beautiful gardens to the hotel's main lobby from where there is a wonderful view of the hotel complex with its many levels set against a backdrop of pools, fountains and delightful Balinese statuary. The hotel offers 5 star luxury and even though an American President (Ronald Reagan) and film stars have stayed there the prices are still reasonable.

Sanur beach

Next door is the more gregarious Club Med property while outside the gates the Nusa Dua village has developed to provide the various ancillary services one always finds in a holiday resort.

The beaches are good and all the normal water sports are available.

> **INFOTIP:** Despite their reputation for free-thinking ideas regarding sex, the Balinese are still offended by the behaviour of foreigners in this regard. Please remember nude or topless bathing is considered offensive and will bring prosecution.

If staying at Nusa Dua it is worth taking the small road that runs east down by the side of Club Med to **Benoa village**. The road, unlike the highway, is narrow, bumpy and rutted but it passes through some interesting small villages with their tiny, local temples. The construction sites of newly planned hotels that will soon change the sleepy nature of the area.

Benoa itself is a most pleasant little fishing hamlet with a scattering of houses, a temple, a police station and a couple of very good seafood restaurants on the beach-front. It is also a centre for para-sailing and snorkelling and makes for a break away from the busier beach further along at Nusa Dua.

Candi Dasa

Candi Dasa (pron. 'Chandi') is the alternative beach resort. It is for those who wish to escape from other tourists and yet still have reasonable facilities.

A two-hour drive from Denpasar midway up the East coast of Bali and still relatively unknown, Candi Dasa is far enough away to deter the average holiday-maker, so one can enjoy a peaceful beach vacation although it lacks the surf of Kuta and the placid swimming of Sanur. In fact the beach itself all but disappears at high tide and it has been necessary to build ugly concrete piers to prevent further erosion of the sand.

Candi Dasa still retains the air of the quiet fishing village it has always been. It seems appropriate the first accommodation for visitors was the **Ghandi Ashrama** where the guests would stay to meditate, practise yoga and partake of strictly vegetarian meals.

Even with the sprouting of various 'home stays', a modern hotel, restaurants and some token shops, the impact on the lifestyle has not been dramatic and there is pleasantly casual approach to life that is not always evident at Kuta or Sanur.

The main features of Candi Dasa is a sea-filled lagoon whose still waters are separated from the ocean by a small peninsula of land with several thatched cottages and tall coconut palms providing the best photo opportunity in the village. And to get the finest pictures it is worth climbing the steep steps of the main temple on the opposite side of the road to the lagoon.

The temple is built on three levels with the two-tiered, outer court-yard starting at street level while there are 78 steps up the precipitous side of the hill to the upper and inner court-yard. From here there are excellent views over the lagoon, to the small islands just off-shore and to Lombok on the horizon. There is also a track that leads into the terraced fields on the hillside.

Supposedly there is a cave that links the temple with the sacred **Mt. Agung** but there is certainly no obvious sign and sounds suspiciously like a local legend.

If nothing else Candi Dasa is a good base from which to visit Bali's most interesting village - **Tenganan**.

Tenganan

Just as you enter Candi Dasa from Denpasar there is a turn-off to the left heading inland. This road will take you to **Tenagan** and into Bali's past, albeit with the trappings of the 20th. century.

The drive to the village is through thick jungle that overhangs the road to form a cooling canopy. Nestled amidst the bamboo thickets and coconut palms are small homes, more and more of which seem to have changed from the original Balinese to the Western bungalow style.

After passing through a couple of minor villages the road ends at a small parking lot, a concession to the tourist who has found Tenganan and is forcing the inevitable changes.

It is pointless to deplore this as the people of Tenganan have as much right to the advantages and disadvantages of tourism as the rest of Bali especially as the economy has changed to emphasise the reliance the island places on the tourist dollar.

Nevertheless Tenganan still maintains a distinct dichotomy with the old rituals and mores being preserved separately while other features are adapted to cater for the visitors and generate income for the village.

The appeal of Tenganan is its status as a **Bali Aga** settlement, a reference to the original 'pure' Indonesian race who once inhabited the island in ancient times and whose descendants remain as a self-centred, conservative community that, until recently, kept itself socially and economically isolated from the rest of the Balinese people.

Tenganan is one of several Bali Aga villages on the island and is the most accessible.

The Bali Aga people secluded themselves behind secure walls, practised their own rites and kept a purity of race by forbidding marriage with those outside the village; offenders were banished and forced to live in homes beyond the village walls.

Visitors were discouraged by active ostracism or by simple, naive methods such as making the gates into the village few and narrow and thus difficult to negotiate. For many years a villager was designated to sweep the village after a visitor left, to wipe out all signs of his presence.

Tenganan is an extensive village attractively laid out in four rows of homes, public buildings and temples on wide, gently terraced slopes of a valley between the dark, steep mountains.

There is wonderful legend as to why Tenganan is so spread out. According to the story the determination of the village's area goes back to the 14th. century when the Tenganan people, who came from **Bedulu**, named for the **king Dalem Bedaulu**, went out on a mission to find the lost and much loved horse of the king. They found the horse although the animal was dead. Nevertheless the king was so pleased he offered to grant them a wish. The wily village chief asked for as much land as would be within an area in which one could smell the dead horse. The king sent a court official with a keen nose to supervise the plotting of the land. This official followed the village chief all day long sniffing in the less than fragrant aroma of the rotting equine corpse. Tired and somewhat surprised that the smell could cover such a distance the official conceded at the end of the day a large tract of land to the Tenganan people. When he left to return to the king with his report the village chief removed from the folds of his clothing a piece of putrid horse meat which he had carried with him throughout the day, so cleverly ensuring the village obtained the widest area of land possible.

Visitors will find Tenganan spotless and well laid out.

The most unusual feature are tall ferris wheel structures on which the local kiddies play but which form an important part of ceremonial dances. Women are suspended on the wheels and rotated during ritual functions.

The Bali Aga rites also require an annual **redjang dance** of the virgins of the village and the young men. This takes on the steps of a formalised mating dance performed to the sound of the **gamelan selunding**, an orchestra composed of oversized gamelan instruments made of large iron plates and struck with huge wooden hammers.

Gamelan orchestra

A more aggressive ritual is that of the festival of **Usaba Sambah** during which two male opponents will fight each other with pandanus leaves with thorns. Although the combatants have plaited shields and the fight is supposed to be a pantomime apparently it becomes an occasion on which to settle old scores and blood is often spilt.

Many of the village homes are now showrooms for a display of the tie-dyed cloths. In Tenganan they practise a method not used elsewhere. It is called **gringsing** and involves the dyeing of both the weft and the warp threads before being woven. There is also a kamben gringsing woven here which is reputed to protect the wearer from black magic.

There are also several craftsmen who make palm leaf books. Painstakingly they etch stories from the **Ramayana** or the Balinese calendar on strips of hard palm leaf which are 'bound' to form an unusual manuscript. But don't expect these books to be cheap. The better ones are quite expensive but are certainly different to anything else you'll see in Bali.

This combination of singular crafts, a unique history and a charming location put Tenganan high on the list of important sights. Hopefully the fact it is off the general tourist track will help preserve its old traditions and that it doesn't succumb any further to modern pressures.

Tanah Lot

North-west of Kuta is the sea temple of Tanah Lot, in the **Tabanan Regency**, and certainly the most popular temple in the southern region for visitors.

The design of the temple and its unique, photogenic location make Tanah Lot a must on tour itineraries.

A decade ago one could wander down a dusty track through the open fields and, at low tide, cross over the rocks to the temple which is set on its own rocky outcrop in the sea.

Today the dusty track is a paved road and after running the gauntlet of souvenir and food stalls the visitor can take his position on the ranks of ugly concrete steps to view the temple from the shore. Access to Tanah Lot itself is no longer allowed due to the wear and tear of the constant stream of visitors along with the natural erosion that is taking place due to the action of the sea (concrete pillars have been erected as breakwaters to lessen the impact of the waves that pound in from the Western waters of the Indonesian Ocean).

Tanah Lot, which is one of several sea temples along the south coast of Bali, dates back to the 16th. century and is believed to have been inspired by the priest, **Danghyang**

Nirartha who had fled from the **Royal Court Blambangan** in Java at the end of the 15th. century to escape the amorous advances of one of the royal wives. On his journeys across Bali, which are interwoven into the myths of the island, **Nirartha** came to this area on the coast where he stopped to rest and meditate. The local people gathered at the feet of this famous holy-man to hear his stories and his philosophy and to be healed of their ailments. Apparently Nirartha preferred to spend the nights on the small island close to the shore rather than in the village itself so when they decided to show their thanks and their respect the villagers felt the island was the ideal site on which to build this temple which they referred to as tengah laut or 'in the middle of the sea' which then derived into **Pura Tanah Lot**.

Sunset is the ideal time to see Tanah Lot when it becomes a dramatic silhouette against the sinking sun in the West. However this is also the most popular time for the tourists who flock in by coach-loads so you may prefer to hire a driver and go early in the morning to contemplate Tanah Lot in solitude and quiet.

Mengwi

It is well worth combining a trip to Tanah Lot with a side journey to Mengwi which is inland to the north. Once again the attraction is a temple and while one can easily be satiated with temples, the peacefulness of Mengwi and the charming setting amidst the cool rain forests provide a pleasant experience.

Until the turn of the century Mengwi was the capital of the major kingdoms of the **Gelgel dynasty**. As such it also was home to one of the major state temples in which the court and the people worshipped the royal ancestors.

The temple is called **Pura Taman Ayun** the word Taman meaning 'a garden with a pond' referring to the pond or moat which is part of the temple complex.

From the roadside entrance through the carved gates, the temple complex rises in a series of wide terraces with beautifully kept lawns and gardens.

Within the last courtyard are a number of merus, the tall temple structures with a series of thatched roofs which increase in number with each separate temple.

Mango trees and a fine bell tower together with excellently preserved buildings help to make this the loveliest temple in Bali.

The three most important gods in particular are worshipped here: **Shiva, Vishnu and Rama** (or Siwa, Wisnu and Rama). The Mengwi temple dates from 1634 but owes its present excellent condition to restoration work carried out in the 1930's.

Blayu

Blayu is a few kilometres to the north-west of Mengwi on the road to **Marga** and is noted for the weaving done in the small village. The local women band together in a cottage industry using bamboo looms. Using tie-dyed threads and gold embroidery they produce many of the songkets,the sarong-like garment used in official ceremonies. An unusual aspect of the cloth they make is the method of cleaning: as it cannot be washed it is cleaned by dusting the material and then hanging it in the sun.

It is easy to miss Blayu as it looks like just another village and it is not on the regular tourist itinerary, however if you are going to Marga then do stop off and browse through the village.

Marga

Marga is a hamlet important to the Balinese for it's place in modern history.

Further north of **Blayu** in **Tabanan Regency**, Marga was the site of the battle of 20th. November 1946 when the modern Balinese hero, Brigadier General I. **Gusti Ngurah Rai**, after whom the international airport is named, died along with all of his 93 guerilla fighters in a bitter battle with a vast Dutch force using both land and air bombardment. This fight to the death was in the tradition of the suicidal puputans of previous decades.

Rows of stone memorials commemorating each of the fighters along with a taller monument to **Ngurah Rai** fill a field in Marga which becomes the scene of an annual march and service.

Sangeh ('monkey forest')

According to the Hindu mythological, epic poem, **Ramayana**, when the monkey general **Hanuman** came to the aid of Rama in his battle with the evil **Rawana**, king of **Lankah**, Hanuman found it was impossible to kill Rawana by normal means. However by crushing him between the two halves of the sacred mountain, **Mahameru** (which became the two mountains **Agung** and **Batur**), he could achieve the demise of Rawana. In so doing a chunk of the mountain containing monkeys of Hanuman's monkey army fell to earth and produced Sangeh, the **Monkey Forest**. Sangeh can be reached by a direct road north from Denpasar. While it is noted for its 17th. century

Balinese performer using gamelan instrument

Mas is the home of the wood carving craft in Bali and Ida Bagus Tilem is its most noted and most talented practitioner, himself the son of another master carver, **Ida Bagus Nyana** who has been recognised officially by the government for the contribution he made to developing the skill of this exacting trade.

The first time I visited his craft shop it was a small, typically Balinese, open-fronted stall. Nowadays he works and sells from two-storied, air-conditioned premises whose large glass windows allow the tall, bamboo thickets to appear as though they were growing inside while trickling streams bonsai-style gardens add a further delightful touch.

The work here is excellent and is reflected in the prices. The superbly executed wooden sculptures are as different from the cheap and crude carvings hawked along the beach at Sanur as a Great Master is different from a hack painter.

There is also a fine selection of ornate and extremely heavy furniture which can be shipped around the world. However you will need a good line of credit and an understanding bank manager. Well worth seeing are the tables whose glass tops cover fascinating tableaux of Balinese life. The amount of detail in each table is amazing.

Barong dance character

Mas also has links with Bali's history as the priest **Danghyang Nirartha** settled here when he fled from Java in the 15th. century.

Although the name Mas means 'gold', it is the woodwork which has won fame for the village. Fine wood carvings were once reserved for the royal courts and for religious purposes but that changed this century.

Ebony is used for much of the work while the fine, gloss of the wood is emphasised with, of all things, ordinary shoe polish.

In the back workrooms you will often find small groups of youthful apprentices carving pieces under the strict eye of a master.

As the village is devoted to this craft it is worth wandering through the small home-cum-workshops and comparing the different levels of skill. Sometimes there is the pleasant surprise of finding a carver who turns out a particularly individual piece away from the normal mould of table boxes, vases and animals.

INFOTIP: Not all craftwork is either cheap or good. Wooden carvings hawked along the beachfront are cheaply mass-produced and of inferior skill and quality. The craft vilage of **Mas** has the best work and is worth a visit.

Ubud temple

Ubud

Of the three main craft villages Ubud is the most charming and the one that would handsomely repay a lengthy stay with a revealing insight into rural Bali. Its ideal for those who wish to escape the well-trod tourist route to **Sanur** and **Kuta**.

Although noted as the home of Bali's artistic colony, Ubud was once the centre of herbal medicine prepared from the herbs that grew in the nearby forest. Hence the name which is an adaptation of 'Ubad' or 'medicine'.

The road from Denpasar enters Ubud at what is basically a T intersection as the road straight ahead narrows and comes to a dead end. The main road continues to the left going through the major part of the village, dipping down to the bridge over the steep **Campuhan gorge** before climbing up the hill again and traversing a ridge with the gorge on one side and the deep green, rice paddies on the other.

At the intersection of the Denpasar and Ubud roads, as elsewhere in Bali, is the chief temple, the **Royal Puri Ubud** with a community hall and open theatre on the other corner. Diagonally across from the temple and running along the road to the right from the intersection is the **Ubud market**.

This is a wonderfully colourful market and is best seen in the morning before the heat of noon-time. In Balinese fashion the stalls are run by women. Their customers, with baskets and parcels balanced on their heads, negotiate the

Ubud, temple

narrow and muddy walk-ways selecting from the baskets of fruits, vegetables and spices. Clothing, thongs and general kitchen requirements are also stocked in the market which has several sections spread over different levels. There is a roofed shopping complex of more permanent stalls, two levels of transient stall-holders and a lower level where the pigs and ducks are sold. The noise is a constant babble of negotiating punctuated by the amplified voice of the story-teller who enthrals the youngsters, and many an older person as well, with some dramatic story using as a prop a tatty old stuffed mongoose which has seen better days, or years for that matter.

In the lower levels small groups of men can be seen sitting with their pet fighting roosters quietly discussing the forthcoming cock fights and the militant capabilities of their individual birds. It is common practise for the proud owners to parade the cocks along the streets of the village each morning to give them a chance to 'see the passing parade' as they claim, tongue in cheek.

Heading north in the opposite direction, just past the temple **Puri Ubud**, is the first of the two largest art galleries, the **Puri Lukisan Museum** which is reached by a bridge over the gorge and a climb up the opposite side of the hill. This has a fine collection of indigenous paintings but the more interesting pieces are to be found a couple of kilometres away in the private collection of **Sutya Neka** which he donated to a small museum which bears his name. Here the works are more representative of the different styles of Balinese art together with a sampling of the Western expatriates who instilled a new sophistication into the local art scene; names like the legendary Walter Spies, Hochler. Donald Friend and Rudolph Bonnet.

There are a several excellent craft shops selling artifacts from both Bali and Lombok and of course there are a myriad of small art shops run by the artists themselves. Many are young and produce paintings in what is known as the 'Young Artists' style which embraces a more vivid use of colour as opposed to the subtle tonings of the older school. A lot of the work is pretty dreadful but there are some interesting selections that would please those who rather fancy the 'Naive' school of art. Ubud is an excellent place to stay and there is a good range of accommodation. A typical example are the Ananda Cottages up on the ridge about a kilometre to the north of the village proper and close to the Sutya Neka Museum. The two story cottages are set in landscaped, terraced gardens amongst the rice fields. It is best to get one of the upper rooms which are bamboo walled and bamboo thatched with two sides open to the air. On drowsy, sunny afternoons there is an idyllic peace sitting there with the soft breezes stirring the bamboo blinds and watching the lazy pace of life in the rice fields as the farmers tend their crops and the lines of obedient ducks waddle after the duck boy with his white flag, which the ducks are trained to recognise and follow.

The days here pass in a pleasant haze of indolence. Meals are taken on an open-air patio as a gamelan player softly provides liquid notes in the background while the surrounding countryside and the village offer wonderful walks. And apart from the brief moments in the morning and the afternoon when the tourist coaches briefly halt on their frantic journeys elsewhere, the tranquil pace of the village is basically unsullied by invading tourist hordes.

Peliatan

This small village to the East of Ubud has a name for its gamelan players and the legong dance troupes. Movie trivia buffs will be interested to know the village produced the first Balinese dance troupe to tour abroad during which time they went to Hollywood to appear in 'The Road to Bali' with Bing Crosby, Dorothy Lamour and Bob Hope. The dancers would have been the only genuine Balinese item in the movie which was filmed entirely on the sound stages of Paramount Pictures in Hollywood.

Goa Gajah

Goa Gajah is the famous **'Elephant Cave'** a name given either because the statue of the **god Ganesa** inside the cave looks like an elephant or because the nearby river **Petanu** was known in olden times as the 'Elephant River'.

In **Gianyar Regency** and not far from the small, royal town of Bedulu, the Goa Gajah was found in 1923 with restoration work in 1954 excavating the bathing pools with water spouting from female statues.

The cave is reached with a climb down the hillside after leaving the coach which is inevitably parked on the opposite side of the road by the line of basket-ware and leather-goods shops.

Over the entrance to the 11th. century cave is a monstrous head with the mouth forming the opening. Depending on the guide's version of the story, this head is either an evil **Kala**, the guardian **Bhoma** or **Pasupati** the god who had divided the mountain **Mahameru** with his bare hands and placed them on the island where they became **Mt. Agung** and **Mt. Batur**. A torch is needed to light the cave's inside passage which is rather short before it meets a T-intersection. In one direction the passage ends at a niche containing the statue of a 3-headed elephant while in the opposite direction the niche contains male genitalia.

The exterior of the Goa Gajah is worth examining for the riotous carvings that adorn the stone cliff face.

Bedulu

Apart from an 11th. century temple the village of Bedulu is of interest because of the fanciful legend surrounding the **Dalem Bedaulu** who ruled during the 14th. century.

The story tells of his magical ability to have a servant decapitate him and then replace the head in working order. However one day jealous gods bewitched the servant into dropping the head into the river. The quick-thinking servant, realising his own head was on the line, immediately beheaded a pig and substituted the porcine cranium on the king's bonce-less neck. From then on the king was forced to rule looking like a cartoon character but managed to conceal the misfortune from most of his subjects by instituting a law forbidding them to look on his countenance.

Blahbatuh

This is a small market village on the road to **Gianyar** and is notable for its gamelan makers and for the carved stone head in the local temple. The head is said to have the features of the **Kebo Iwa** who had a reputation for great strength and magical powers. The town also has a small palace with a fine collection of orchids.

Gianyar

Gianyar is the administrative centre for the Regency of the same name and, as such, is a town of considerable size. It also has a deal of charm as the various government and regional buildings are neat in design and the wide road through the centre of town is divided by a median strip with flower beds.

The name is believed to be a corruption of two words: **Griya** or 'priest's house' and **Anyar** or 'new'.

Opposite the town square with its decorative statue of a rearing white horse is the local palace. Its high, decorative walls hide the main buildings which were once the centre of a powerful kingdom during the 18th. century only to have the power taken away through mis-management a hundred years later.

Gianyar is the site of many textile factories producing large numbers of everyday sarongs. It is also famous for its **Babi Guling**, the roast suckling pig which is a great

main intersection. On the ceiling of the court-room is a large mural depicting the torments of hell for all transgressors of the law. Many a nervous eye has been cast upwards while waiting a verdict from the judges of the court. Adjoining this building is the **Bale Kambang**, the **Floating Pavilion** which also has many distinctive paintings.

When it comes to paintings it is worth a visit two kilometres south of Klungkung to **Kamesan** where the wayang style of painting was developed from the symbolism of the puppet shadow plays and using themes from the Ramayana and various Javanese classics. Kamesan also produces fine silver and gold craft-work which is for sale in the shops of Klungkung.

To the east of Klungkung on the road to **Candi Dasa** as the road leaves the **Undu River** and skirts the coastline the remnants of the disastrous 1963 volcanic upheaval of Mt. Agung are still in evidence. Villagers can be seen fossicking along the line of the lava flow looking for lava stones which they sell.

Ubud temple

School children on bicycles

Tampaksiring

Tampaksiring, the site of the holy springs, is usually combined with a tour to the craft centres of Celuk, Mas and Ubud and provides an agreeable contrast to these busy villages, although having to face the hawkers outside the springs, one may think otherwise.

The holy springs of **Tirta Empul** are just outside the village of Tampaksiring and is reached by a road that branches one way to the springs while the other leads to the Presidential summer house which was particularly favoured by the late **President Soekarno**. Locals like to tell of members of the presidential staff using binoculars to spy on the young women bathing in the pools below.

The site was established as a sacred centre in 962 A.D. with the temple of Tirta Empul being built over the source of the springs which, according to mythology, were created by Indra to revive those gods poisoned at **Sukawati** by **Mayadanawa**. The waters were believed to bestow immortality.

From spouts in the temple the water flows into bathing pools which have been carefully divided into areas for men and women and with a special pool for menstruating women (although a sign spells out the ban on such women from entering the temple). Visitors will be required to don a temple sash before entering the sacred precincts and, as with all religious sites, conservative dress is required which usually means covered arms and legs for women but not necessarily for men (the logic of that is never clearly explained).

Lake Kintamani, boats for rent

Penelokan _____

After leaving Tampaksiring the road north winds up the hills of northern Bali until it intersects with the road from **Bangli** at the village of Penelokan.

Not for nothing does the name Penelokan translate into 'the place of looking', for it is here you get your first view of Mt. Batur and **Lake Batur**.

Penelokan is on the rim of a giant crater containing Mt. Batur and the lake and the views across to the smoking volcano and the lava-clad slopes down to the lake are breathtaking.

Accommodation here is basically of the losmen style with standard, cheap rooms. But the view compensates for the lack of 5 star facilities and the village is a good base for those who would like to spend a few days and explore the lake and the mountain. If staying then it is wise to take the traditional siesta around noon and avoid the coach-loads of day trippers who arrive here for the luncheon break.

From Penelokan a road winds down the hillside to the lake village of **Keidisan**. From here you can take walking tours along the lake and up to the crater of Mt. Batur or sail across the lake to the introverted village of **Trunyan**. Trunyan is one of the original Bali Aga villages where they live an isolated existence and do not put out the welcome mat for visitors as in the other Bali Aga village of **Tenganan**. So expect a surly greeting but at least you will be spared the hawkers.

Batur

Between Penelokan and Kintamani, this 'official' village of Batur is quite small but is the site of an impressive temple complex. Since the volcanic eruption of 1926, the villagers have been re-building and extending the **Puru Ulun Danu** which was moved here from the foot of Mt. Batur to escape the lava flows. Nearly 300 shrines are planned for the whole compound.

Kintamani

This village gives its name to the daily Kintamani Tour from Denpasar which takes in the craft villages, Tampaksiring and this township perched on the rim of the crater further round from Penelokan.

The coach tours stop here for lunch which can be taken at one of the many restaurants in the village although, as an alternative, it is worth considering those in Penelokan or those you pass along the road. However nothing you do can protect you from the hordes of hawkers who seem to be at their most bothersome at Kintamani. Anyone trying to have a private picnic out of sight will find that some instinctive homing device has the postcard, batik and statue sellers swarming within minutes like the proverbial bees to a honey-pot. Luckily the government has realised how off-putting this is for tourists and has instituted a programme to persuade the locals that a less intrusive approach will pay bigger dividends.

Every three days there is a major market held in Kintamani.

To the east providing yet another impressive backdrop is the silhouette of the sacred Mt. Agung.

Besakih and Mt.Agung

The Besakih tour is a day-long trip in itself and is too distant to combine it with the Kintamani tour.

Culturally and religiously this is the most important part of Bali for Besakih, on the side of Mt. Agung, is the mother temple of the Balinese people while the mountain itself is so tied in with the religion and the sociology of Bali as to determine the complete mode of living for the people whose homes and even streets are laid out in deference to the mountain.

The road from Klungkung climbs up the hills through the village of **Bukit Jamul** where there is a splendid vista of mountains and cool, green valleys. A restaurant on the high side of the road provides necessary refreshments to accompany the view.

BALI MANDIRA COTTAGES
Jl. Padma, Kuta.
Phone : 0361-51381
96 rooms.
R-B-AC-BT

BALI RANI
Jl. Kartika, Kuta.
P.O. Box. 1034, Tuban.
Phone : 0361-51369
50 rooms.
R-B-AC-HT

BALI SANUR BUNGALOWS
Jl. Raya Sanur, Sanur.
P.O. Box 306, Denpasar.
Phone : 0361-8421/2
387 rooms.
R-B-AC-HT

BRUNA BEACH INN
JL. Melasti, Legian.
Phone : 0361-51564/5
26 rooms.
R-B-AC-BT

CLUB BUALA
Nusa Dua.
P.O. Box. 6, Nusa Dua
Phone : 0361-71310
50 rooms
R-B-AC-BT

DENPASAR
Jl. Diponegoro 103, Denpasar.
Phone : 0361-26336
66 rooms.
R-B-AC-HT-BT

DHARMA WISATA
Jl. Imam Bonjol 89, Denpasar.
Phone : 0361-22186
31 rooms.

DHYANA PURA
Jl. Dhyana Pura, Banjar Seminyak
Kuta.
Phone : 0361-51442/3, 51462
40 rooms.
R-B-AC-BT-HT

DIWANGKARA BEACH
Jl. Raya Sanur, Sanur.
P.O. Box 120, Denpasar.
Phone : 0361-8577
36 rooms.
R-B-AC-HT

FOURTEEN ROSES
Jl. Raya Legian,Kuta.
Phone : 0361-51156
20 rooms.

GAZEBO COTTAGES
Jl. Tanjung Sari, Sanur,
P.O. Box 134, Denpasar.
Phone : 0361-8300
60 rooms.
R-B-AC

GOLDEN VILLAGE INN
Jl. Raya Legian, Kuta.
P.O. Box.116
22 rooms.
BT

KARTIKA PLAZA
Jl. Kartika, Kuta.
P.O. Box. 84, Denpasar.
Phone : 0361-51067/8/9
120 rooms.
R-B-AC-BT

KUTA VILLAGE INN
Jl. Bakung Sari, Kuta.
Phone : 0361-1795, 51724
30 rooms.
R-B-AC-HT

KUTA BEACH CLUB
Jl. Bakung Sari, Kuta.
Phone : 0361-51261/2
96 rooms.
R-B-AC-HT-BT

KUTA BEACH NATOUR
Jl. Patai Kuta No. 1
P.O. Box. 393, Denpasar.
Phone : 0361-51461/2
35 rooms.
R-B-AC-BT

Accommodation

SINAR BEACH COTTAGES
Jl. Pura Bagus Teruna Legian, Kuta.
16 rooms.
R-B-AC

SINDHU BEACH
Jl. Pantai Sindhu, Sanur.
P.O. Box 181, Denpasar.
Phone: 0361-8351/2
50 rooms.
R-B-AC-HT-BT

WINA COTTAGES
Br. Pengabetan, Kuta.
Phone: 0361-51867
78 rooms.
R-B-AC-BT

SARI YASA SAMUDRA BUNGALOWS
Jl. Pantai, Kuta.
Phone: 0361-51562
30 rooms.
R-B-AC-BT

SEGARA VILLAGE
Jl. Segara Ayu, Sanur.
Phone: 0361-8407/8, 8021/2
110 rooms. HT: 19 & BT: 91.
R-B-AC-HT-BT

YULIA BEACH INN
Jl. Pantai Kuta.
Phone: 0361-51055, 51862
48 rooms.

Bali Beach Hotel pool area

ADVANCE PLANNING

If you need additional information when preparing your itinerary then contact the Indonesian consulate or Garuda Indonesian Airlines office in major cities or write direct to the Bali Government Tourism Office (Jl. Raya Puputan, Niti Mandala, Renon, Denpasar. Phone: 0361-22387). The BGTO can provide pamphlets, maps and up to date information that will be useful in planning a budget or making bookings.

What to bring

Documents: Passport, valid for at least six months. Insurance documents, an international driving license, credit cards and any relevant student cards. If you have business cards take a plentiful supply as the exchange of cards in Asia is almost a pre-requisite for doing business. Even on holiday it is handy to carry a few cards.

Clothing: Light weight informal clothing is generally the rule for Bali's humid climate, however, for visits to official offices and other formal occasions a jacket and tie will be required (some government offices will refuse to serve those who are improperly dressed). Special consideration should be given to local standards of appearance especially when in villages or visiting places of worship. It is necessary for both men and women to wear sashes around their waists when entering temples or attending ceremonies. Shorts and halter-tops should not be worn in temples. Despite the frankness with which the Balinese people approach the subject of sex they are still a modest race and for that reason nude bathing is considered offensive and is illegal.

Odds and Ends: The following items are available in Bali, but you may wish to bring your own to save the time and effort of looking for them: Towels, for swimming and hair; (with the exception of the larger international hotels, the average Balinese hotel towel will barely dry a gnat); extra hangers; plastic bags for wet clothes when travelling (the humidity means wet items take a long time to dry); a traveller's clothesline; pins; a universal bath plug. Also remember to bring extra glasses (normal prescription glasses if you wear them and sunglasses), contact lenses, medicines, prescriptions, sunscreen ointment. However

Practical Information

Denpasar, Kuta and Sanur have a good range of shops and pharmacies and most normal household items are readily obtainable.

Entry Regulations

Tourist visas are not required for the following countries: Australia, Austria, Belgium, Brunei, Canada, Denmark, Finland, France, Greece, Iceland, Ireland, Italy, Japan, Lichtenstein, Luxemburg, Malaysia, Netherlands, New Zealand, Norway, Philippines, Singapore, South Korea, Spain, Sweden, Switzerland, Thailand, United Kingdom, U.S.A. and West Germany. Holders of passports for these countries may enter Indonesia for tourist purposes for a stay of no more than two months. For tourists from other countries a 30 day visa can be obtained upon application at a relevant Indonesian consulate.

For travel to some out of the way places in Indonesia special Domestic Travel Permits are required. However this is rare in Bali but should you be planning to get 'off the beaten track' check with the nearest Police station whether such travel is permitted and to register your route so a search can be mounted if you get lost.

> **INFOTIP:** A course of anti-malaria tablets prior to your Bali holiday is a good precaution. And don't forget the insect repellents.

Customs

You will be permitted to bring with you: 2 litres of alcohol; 200 cigarettes or 50 cigars or 100 grams of tobacco; a 'reasonable' amount of perfume. The following items are permitted on the condition that they are recorded on your arrival and taken with you on departure: photographic, video & filming equipment; cars; and typewriters. The following items are prohibited: narcotics; arms and ammunition; TV sets, radio & radio cassette players; Chinese print material and Chinese medicines. If you wish to use radios, film or video equipment then it is best to seek advice from the appropriate government authorities before departure (these are official instructions but tourists will have no hassle bringing in a radio or cassette player for their own use).

JAPAN
Jalan M H Thamrin 24, Jakarta. Phone: 324308, 324948, 325268
Jalan Raya Sanur Tanjung 123, Denpasar. Phone: 25611.

MALAYSIA
Jalan Imam Bonjol 17, Jakarta. Phone: 336438, 332864.

NETHERLANDS
Jalan H R Rasuna Said, Kav s3, Kuningan, Jakarta.
Phone: 511551.

NEW ZEALAND
Jalan Diponegoro 41, Jakarta. Phone: 330552, 330620, 330680.

NORWAY
4th floor, Bina Mulia Building, Jalan H R Rasuna Said, Kav 10, Jakarta. Phone: 517140, 511990.

PAPUA NEW GUINEA
6th floor, Panin Bank Centre, Jalan Jen Sudirman, Jakarta. Phone: 711218, 711225/6.

PHILIPPINES
Jalan Imam Bonjol 6-9, Jakarta. Phone: 348917.

SINGAPORE
Jalan Proklamasi 23, Jakarta. Phone: 348761, 347783.

SRI LANKA
Jalan Diponegoro 70, Jakarta. Phone: 321018, 321896.

SWEDEN
Jalan Taman Cut Mutiah 12, Jakarta. Phone: 333061
Segara Village Hotel, Jalan Segara, Sanur, Phone: 8231, 8407.

THAILAND Jalan Imam Bonjol 74, Jakarta.
Phone: 343762, 349180.

UK Jalan M H Thamrin 75, Jakarta. Phone: 330904.

USA Jalan Medan Merdeka Selatan 5, Jakarta.
Phone: 360360.

WEST GERMANY Jalan M H Thamrin 1, Jakarta.
Phone: 323908, 324292, 324357.
17 Jalan Pantai Karang, Sanur. Phone: 8535.

Death

The death of a foreign citizen requires instant consultation with her or his Consulate by friends, relatives, hospital or police authorities. Airlines will be particularly helpful in arranging for the body to be returned home. It is imperative your insurance policy covers this eventuality (many policies will also provide for a companion to be flown out to escort a sick person home).

Lost Property or Theft

The following may help you replace your lost or stolen property. Report serious loss or theft immediately. Even if your property cannot be recovered, the record will be needed to replace documents, tickets, travellers' checks, or to claim insurance. If possible get a translation of the police statement into your own languate or at least into English.

Loss or theft of ID, passports etc. should be reported to the police and to your consulate.

If necessary advertise any lost property in the local papers. Leave valuable items such as passports, airline tickets and excess cash and travellers cheque in the hotel safe. If none is available rent a safety deposit box at the local bank. Otherwise a money belt strapped to the body is the next best safeguard. When carry a handbag, purse or wallet do not hold it on the road side of the pavement when walking....it is too easy to grab from a passing bike. Never carry a wallet in your back-pocket. Do not display large sums of money in public places.

Replacement of Certain Items

Airline Tickets: Report the loss/theft to the airline and request replacement. A copy of the police report should be presented to the airline. Replacements can usually be issued only after the complete ticket information has been provided, and verification of your lost ticket obtained from the issuing office. With youth fare tickets you will probably have to buy a new ticket and obtain refund at the issuing office.

Credit Cards: Report loss immediately to the credit card company.

Driving Licenses: Consult your Consulate for advice.

Passport: Report immediately to your consulate within working hours.

Student Cards: Contact the International Youth Travel Service. You must have a valid university or college ID card.

Travellers' Cheques: Issuing firms normally replace these quickly upon proof of purchase together with details of those already cashed. Before leaving home check the addresses of the local offices of the firm supplying the cheques. Some credit card companies can offer emergency cash supplies upon production of the credit card.

It is a good idea to keep the numbers of your travellers cheques and airline tickets in a separate place. Leave a set of the numbers at home in a readily accessible place so that a phone call can give you the numbers if required.

CRIME

Crime is of little consequence in Bali with visitors being free to wander at will. However in crowded market places pickpockets are active and valuables should be left in the hotel safe. Cash is best carried in money belts. The Balinese authorities have strict laws regarding the use of drugs and Westerners caught in possession will suffer the same penalties as local residents (the local Depansar gaol is not noted for its cuisine or facilities!).

EMERGENCIES

Medical Services

Most villages have small government run clinics with qualified doctors and nurses. Apart from the following list there are hospitals to be found in the towns of Bangli, Gianya, Mengwi and Singaraja.

Hospitals

R.S.U.P. Sanglah (Public Hospital), Jl. Diponegoro, Denpasar, Phone: 24141/24142 (24 hours).
R.S. Wangaya (Public Hospital), Jl. Kartina. Denpasar, Phone: 22142.
R.S.A.D. (Army Hospital), Jl. Sudirman, Denpasar, Phone: 26521 (24 hours).
P.M.I. Badung (Red cross Rep.), Jl. Imam Bonjol, Denpasar, Phone: 26305.

> **INFOTIP:** Balinese doctors and hospitals can cope with most medical problems. However if in doubt and if the matter is serious consider repatriation, Djakarta or Australia.

MOTORING

Motoring in and around the major towns is usually chaotic, but once out in the country side the traffic is much lighter. Getting around is not difficult as the roads are well signposted and most of the main roads are reasonably surfaced. It is a good idea to stock up on fuel while in the larger towns as the few service stations that are out in the country are often unreliable.

Driving is on the left hand side of the road with a speed limit of 40 km.p.hr in the towns and 80 km. p. hr. on the open road. Road signs follow the international code.

Car Rental

International car rental companies are well represented in Bali and there is also a thriving private trade which can be far cheaper but may not offer the solace of insurance in case of accident. Check carefully on conditions if hiring privately. Short and long term rentals are available. Another possibility is the long term rental of a Bemo or a Colt minibus with or without driver. To drive you will require an International Driving Permit.

> **INFOTIP:** AVIS ,HERTZ and BUDGET are represented in Bali as well as a wide range of local rental agencies,mostly of the 'one-man , one car' variety. Most owners of *Bemos* or private cars will arrange a deal but may not offer insurance coverage.

Private Cars

The importation of private cars requires special permission and arrangements would need to be made through the Indonesian consulate. However there is no problem with bringing cars already in Indonesia across on the ferry from Java.

SHOPPING

Just about everything in Bali with a price tag is open to bargaining, with the exception of restaurant meals and accommodation (sometimes even accommodation can be bargained down). Most souvenirs and gift items can be reduced in price by up to a half, or even two thirds, of the original. Those shops where the price is fixed will have notices however if trade is slow most shop-keepers will be open to an offer.

INFOTIP: The Balinese have immense charm and honesty. But, as in most countries, Westerner visitors have instilled an unhealthy appreciation of the Almighty Dollara so be prepared to find shrewd, street wise merchants, hawkers and taxi drivers who will charge the highest prices they think they will get away with... often higher than you would pay at home. Unless in a restaurant or shop with marked and fixed prices always haggle.

For airconditioned comfort the arcades in the larger hotels are the best however prices will be dearer. The best bargains are to be found in rural village markets. However the tourist dollar has sparked a rash of tourist shops in the most surprising places. The hawkers at tourist resorts are legendary pests and at any popular destination you will have to run the gauntlet.

INFOTIP: A small, pocket calculator of the type which automatically converts currency is a good investment. This will give you a good idea of the prices you are paying in your own money.

What to buy

BATIK is a traditional form of Indonesian fabric dyeing; patterns are drawn onto the cloth in wax which resists the dye, the wax is then removed and the procedure can be repeated to produce designs of varying complexity. The batik fabric can be seen in the everyday dress of the Balinese. It is possible to buy batik in lengths of fabric or fashioned into shirts, blouses and dresses. However good batik is not cheap.

HANDCRAFTS & ANTIQUES can be found anywhere from the beach markets to the main street shops and galleries. As well as the local Balinese handcrafts the visitor will be able to find items from other parts of Indonesia and artifacts from China including krisses, puppets, bamboo work, bone-carvings, baskets, antique jewelry and Chinese porcelain.

PAINTINGS. Ubud is the home of the Balinese art community; here you will be able to visit the galleries (and homes) of the local and foreign artists. Painting continues to be a dynamic part of the local culture with influences coming from traditional as well as foreign artists.

WOODCARVING is one of the more prominent of local Balinese handcrafts. Ornate sculptures made of indigenous and imported woods can be purchased in shops all over the Island. Antique carvings can be found in Sanur and Klungkung. Many of the pieces hawked along the beach are of poor quality.

GOLD & SILVER WORK. Balinese metal craft makes use of delicate wirework to form ornate boxes and jewelry. Kuta, Celuk and Kamasan are places where you will find smiths producing contemporary gifts and souvenirs, for more traditional work go to Denpasar, Gianyar, Jalan Sulawesi and Kartini.

INFOTIP: Although turtle meat and turtle soup are still to be found on restaurant menus, remember the turtle is an endangered species and the Balinese authorities are conducting a campaign to remind visitors of this.

SPORT AND ATHLETICS

Water Sports

It almost goes without saying that one of the dominant lures for the visitor to Bali is the abundance and quality of water sporting activities. Diving, snorkling, surfing, skiing, sailing, spear fishing, wind surfing, are all well catered for.

Diving Companies

AQUANAUT, Tedjo Express Tours: 24, Jalan W.R.Supprat-man,Denpasar.
Phone: (0361) 28561-3
BALI DIVE SPORTS CLUB, C/-I. Ketut Wetha, Br. Semawang, Sanur,
Denpasar. Phone: (0361) 8582.
BALI MARINE WATER SPORTS, C/-I. Ketut Wiraja, Br. Semawang,
Sanur, Denpasar.
BARUNA WATER SPORTS, Office: Jalan Bypass I Gst Ngurah Rai,
Tuban.
Phone: (0361) 51223-6.
GLORIA MARIS DIVING CLUB, Marina Bali Water Sport: P.O. Box 442
Denpasar, Bali.
Phone: (0361) 23853.

Information on wind surfing can be obtained from:

BALI OPEN BOARD SAILING COMMITTEE, C/- Hotel Segara Village,
Sanur, Bali, Indonesia. Phone: (0361) 8407/8021.

Golf

Golf fans have a choice of two courses, a nine hole course at the Hotel Bali Beach, and an eighteen hole championship course in the central mountains at Bedugul overlooking Lake Bratan. Fees are reasonable and advance bookings are a wise idea.

Tennis

Major hotels at Sanur, Kuta and Nusa Dua usually have courts but as they are normally reserved for guests, non-guests will have to make special arrangements.

TIPPING

Most major hotels and restaurants will automatically add a service charge in addtion to government taxes to a bill. Where no service charge is added, a 10% to 15% tip is now normally expected where good service is given. There is no tipping required for bemo or taxi drivers but a small tip should be given to porters at the airport or at your hotel for carrying your bag. Whilst one deplores the practise Bali has fallen into line with the rest of the world in this matter. For many workers it is the only way supplement meagre wages.

TIME

Bali is on Central Indonesia Standard Time which is GMT 8 hours.

TOURIST SERVICES

The Indonesian flag carrier is Garuda Indonesia which links Bali with Denpasar, Paris, Amsterdam, Vienna, Rome, Zurich, Brussels, Frankfurt, Abu Dhabi, Kuala Lumpur, Singapore, Manila, Hong Kong, Tokyo, Guam, Honolulu, Los Angeles, Melbourne, Sydney, Brisbane, Perth and Darwin. Depending on the aircraft used the carrier offers First Class, Business Class and Economy class. On some internal flights only Economy Class is available and on some DC10 flights only Business and Economy. The fleet consists of Boeing 747's, DC10's, DC9's, Air Bus 300's and Fokker F28's.

Further domestic flights are provided by Merpati Nusantara Airlines using turbo-prop jets.

Tourist Information Centres in Bali

AIRPORT INFORMATION CENTRE
Ngurah Rai International Airport, Tuban. Phone: (0361) 25081, 25083.
BADUNG GOVERNMENT TOURISM OFFICE
Jl. Surapati, Denpasar. Phone: (0361) 23602.
BALI GOVERNMENT TOURISM OFFICE
Jl. Raya Puputan, Niti Mandala, Renon, Denpasar.
Phone: (0361) 22387.
GOVERNMENT TOURISM INFORMATION BUILDING
Jl. Bakung Sari, Kuta. Phone: (0361) 51419. Telex 35276.
TOURIST INFORMATION CENTRE
Jl. Veteran, Singaraja. Phone: 339 Singaraja.
UBUD TOURIST INFORMATION SERVICE
Bina Wisata, Ubud.

THE METRIC SYSTEM

Length

1 millimetre	0.04 inches
1 centimetre	0.39 inches
1 metre	1.09 yards
1 kilometre	0.62 mile

Alphabetical Index

Index

Notes

Notes

Notes